BALI
in its
MIDDLE AGES

Brian Lavery

BALI in its MIDDLE AGES

By Brian Lavery

Copyright © 2024 Brian Lavery

Maroochydore, Queensland, Australia

balipocketbook@blavery.com

ISBN: 978-0648846697

Fiction

Inbound

Everything in this visitor's log is untrue. All these stories and vignettes and snippets. All the characters, all the facts, all the events. None of it happened.

Except that some items, perhaps several, might feel familiar. Some of the things in that island's Middle Ages.

Enjoy the frolic. Add some more plus to your rainbow. And try to re-imagine those earlier days, re-invent those people and places that are gone, and wonder about what water has already moved to sea.

BALI in its MIDDLE AGES

Anne with Gado2

It was on a different island, Berry Island. All islands can be romantic places.

And flattery works well on someone who had led a quiet and unattached life

1988

for some while. One who was nursing a few disappointments.

He found his way to the jazz band playing there and became the immediate new face in that group. Susan, Katherine and Anne took their turns to move closer and to talk. The winning bid went to Anne.

'Jack, so you've been to Bali several times? I have twice, too. Can you speak any Indonesian?'

'A little. Sedikit.'

'Sedikit saja,' Anne repeated, and beamed.

He didn't remember "saja".

'But you can?'

'High school,' she said. 'There were no Japanese classes, so I took Indonesian.'

'Oh, well, I just learned some key words by being over there and learning to cope. It's fun.'

'Hey, listen,' she said. 'I found a great gado-gado place last month in Manly Vale. Would you come with me next week to try it out?'

'OK, You're on. Next week.'

Thursday night they were sitting at Warung Sendok Bali, talking, awaiting their gado-gado.

Anne:

1973 was the end of my School Certificate year. Our prim Mrs Faulding offered to take her language students on an educational experience trip to Java and Bali. Poor woman, she never offered a repeat! I was the youngest to go.

We left Sydney for Indonesia on Boxing Day. The Garuda flight was awful, crowded and smelly. Disgusting. We got there, but it was rather traumatic.

Mrs Faulding had arranged a bus to meet us at Jakarta Airport. We wanted to go to Bali.

Jakarta was busy and noisy and so hot. We were in a big hotel in the city, but lots of things were broken or not working. Doors not closing. Lights that flickered if they did work. At least the toilets were like those at home—not like the funny ones we got everywhere else—but they wouldn't flush properly and had no paper.

And I can remember Bandung. We were in the local movie theatre watching a Chinese Kung Fu movie. We were there to practise reading Indonesian from the subtitles. All fifteen of us streamed into this theatre and sat in one long row, a couple from the front. Then in came a gang of Indonesian boys, and they sat in the seats in front of us. Mrs Faulding was horrified.

But at Yogyakarta we stayed a few nights, and that was different because we were billeted into local houses so we could practice our Indonesian. I liked especially the Buddhist temple at Borobodur. We stayed for hours. Have you been there?

Not yet.

No? Not yet. So you have seen some of Java?

Jakarta, Puncak Pass, the Bogor Gardens, yes. By bus once. Back northwards by overnight train another time, staying up into the night, watching from the train the trillions of fireflies across the paddy fields.

Oh, wow!

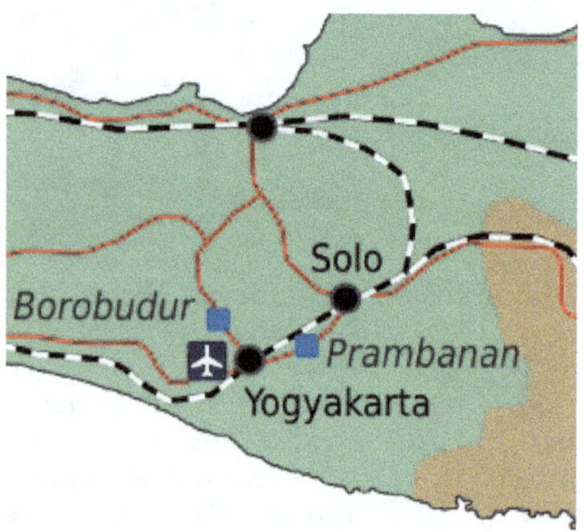

We weren't allowed to drink the water. Still, every day we got a jug of water in our room, but we were afraid of that, too. We'd sneak off and buy bottles of Green Spot, but that wasn't green, it was orange.

BALI in its MIDDLE AGES

Then somehow we jumped out of Java into Bali for the second week. We still had our bus.

We were in a modest hotel in Denpasar, two in a room. We lived there at night but each day we went off somewhere, usually in our bus.

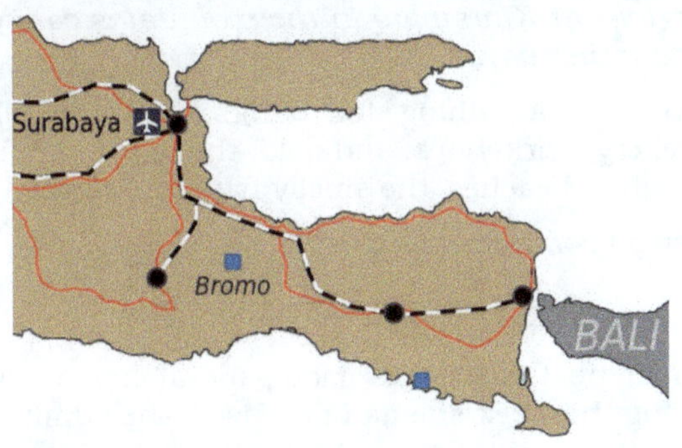

Was Bali easier for the girls?

Oh, yes. We were all so excited to get to Bali. We thought it would be a magic place. In Java we had to use our Indonesian more, but in Bali more people could speak some English words. That made it easier, but Mrs Faulding would hear us and remind us to use Bahasa.

Hey, we are all finished, and the night is getting late. I do need to be up early.

There's one thing I need to tell you. You have the nicest eyes. Now in return you tell me something.

Tell me we can do this again, real soon. Then we can talk more on Bali.

Tell you? OK. Sure, we can do this again. Including Bali.

Thanks. Let's go. The obnoxious sellers of bone carvings at Kintamani in the mountains can wait for another day.

And the bargaining for batiks, and the silver jewellery workshops, and gold, the wood carvings, the white beaches, the smelly fruit, the coral?

How do you know all that?

———

Dinner next week was gado-gado at home. Twice during the week she had practised, she admitted.

'Sit down. Let's eat. Share some Bali stories this time.'

They sat.

Her Bali and his Bali matched at many points. The girls' expedition was shepherded through all the Bali days by a young university graduate, Mbak Ida.

'No, she told us, call me *Miss* Ida.'

Ida spoke both languages well, and had used the mix over the week to introduce her charges to the Bali she loved: Denpasar city and its markets, the temples of Uluwatu, of Tanah Lot, of the ancient

                      BALI in its MIDDLE AGES

Besakih, the "mother temple" complex on the volcano. They saw theatre and dance, Legong at Ubud, the Monkey Dance in Denpasar. And the wood-carvers and the silver-workers north of Denpasar.

'Some of it was rather ethnic, and many of us became tired of so much of it. So then they took us to a forest to see wild monkeys, and that was our favourite story to our families when we got home,' she said.

She left him, and returned with ice cream.

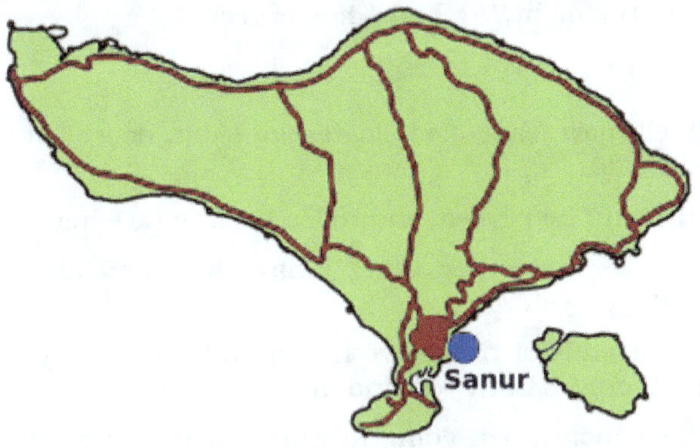

'But I went to Bali a second time. As well as Mrs Faulding's trip in High School, I took my younger sister Dale in 1982, to Sanur. I could show off. I was the experienced one, and I knew the language.'

She sighed.

'We didn't have a good trip. For five of our six days, Dale was sick. Very sick. We were both worried. They called in a skinny Dutch doctor, who gave her some opium tincture pills that helped. So we didn't see much of Bali except for the last day. Still today, when I show Dale the photo of her on that day shrieking at the monkey on the ledge near her, she says she can't remember that. The little skink is all she remembers, that lived up the wall and squawked half the night. We had a house gecko.'

———

'Well, now, that complicates us a bit, doesn't it?' she said.

'Hmmm,' he replied, and rolled back to face her.

'There's one other thing I haven't talked about with you yet.'

Thousands of things we haven't talked about yet, he thought. Both you and me.

'Next month, I'm going to Europe with Katherine for nine weeks.'

He sat up.

　　　　　　　　　　BALI in its MIDDLE AGES

'We've plotted it since last year. We have holidayed away together before, but nothing as huge as this.'

She sat up as well.

'So that's why we have complicated everything.'

'Nothing needs to be complicated,' he said. You go and have the best holiday you can manage. You see new places, you eat other foods, struggle with being understood. You have fun, you get homesick, you spend money.'

'Yeah, but—'

'... and maybe you meet someone exciting and you throw yourself into some wild thing with them. It could be you never come home, even that can happen.'

'No,' she said.

'Yes,' he said. 'And the thing I must say is this. If you come home after all your adventures, whatever they be, and you leap back into my life, I'd be a happy person.'

'No,' she said.

'No?'

'No, that's not the person I am.'

He didn't understand. Understanding took a very long time.

Christy and the Nurse

He didn't belong here. He never would belong, because he wasn't a surfer.

Nor one of those emerging foreign petty entrepreneurs, starting a pub. He wasn't affluent, to afford lavish holidays.

Not a correct fit.

Ben had persuaded him, but Ben wasn't a surfer either. Ben had been to Bali three years ago, homewards from a yoga school at Solo in Java. He was lukewarm now about those yoga classes, thought the madrasah colleges there were alien and hiding something.

Yet Ben enthused over Bali. Kuta. The beach. The people. The food. The foreign, friendly culture. Different foreign.

'Jack,' Ben had said, 'it's time you travelled, saw places. And Indonesia is our closest neighbour, ten times our population. Get out!'

But Jack had travelled before, to England and Germany on government business, on an official passport. That was the hot British summer of '73, the time of a poor Britain still waiting on the promised North Sea oil to refurbish its ailing economy.

———

Ben told them, both Jack and Christy: don't let the touts inside at the Bali Airport persuade you into their taxi. Don't trust anyone hassling you. Walk out past the taxi area, out beyond the airport proper, and there will be more cars outside. Those will be cheaper.

Anxious, they exited the airport. But there they were, more taxis and cars. He accepted the first one. He counted out what the driver asked.

The taxi let them off twenty minutes later. 'Kuta. Bemo Corner,' said the driver.

The large road junction was dusty and unsealed, and a scrappy tree stood in the middle, supporting a stonework stand and a noticeboard. That made the intersection a road roundabout, he decided. But the minimal traffic ignored that and went either way around the centre tree.

'Blimey, it's hot,' said Christy, standing in the dust.

They sat down on a wooden stool bench in the narrow shade beside a wall. The day was well on, and they shouldn't dally long.

But, 'Look, Coca-Cola,' she said.

Bottled drinks were on sale from a blue hand-cart, and they ordered two Fanta. These were a clear lemonade, not the orange they knew. But they were from a cooler box.

But saying "…ordered two Fanta…" does no justice to how it happened.

'How much should those be?' he said. Christy shrugged.

'How much?' and he pointed to a Coke bottle.

'One thousand.'

                    BALI in its MIDDLE AGES

How much was one thousand? He looked at the notes they had exchanged at the airport an hour ago. It felt a million rupiah. They were rich.

In this country everyone was expected to bargain for all purchases. Ben again.

'Six hundred,' he offered.

The seller was bored. 'One thousand.'

'How much for two of those?' he said, pointing to the Fanta bottles.

'Two thousand rupiah.'

'OK,' he said.

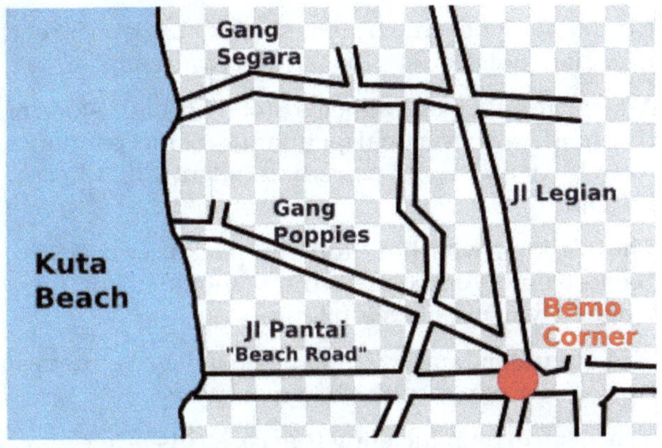

The instructions were to start walking north, up Legian Street. If you pass Gang Poppies, you know you are headed the right way. "Jalan Legian" was signed. The sun was too clouded to decide north otherwise.

By half a kilometre, the tile-roofed shops and the shacks had thinned out, and the side tracks leading westwards toward where the beach should be were empty until a few hundred metres closer to the beach. Several cows roamed to the left among the many coconut trees. The road, of coral, no bitumen, was all dusty.

Neither was admitting to being spooked.

There was no traffic except for one tiny southbound three-wheeled vehicle put-putting along, "Bajaj" branded on its front. From India?

Running along the beach side of Legian Street, they had just a dusty foot trail to walk on.

A large number of flagpoles stood on both sides of the road, with vertical pennants. Some pennants were tatty and some poles had fallen. 'Don't know,' he said.

The walking was hot, and the packs were heavy. 'Jack, would you cope with my shoulder bag for a while? My arm aches a bit.'

The shoulder bags were cabin baggage, a modest weight compared to the backpacks.

'Yeah, sure, help me sling it across this other way.'

A large and noisy motorbike passed them going north. The pillion had her long, blonde hair blowing in the air. Along the length of the bike,

    BALI in its MIDDLE AGES

and longer than the bike, was mounted a surfboard. Other than the motorbike, the only traffic was a few locals walking or bicycling south towards Kuta.

'Why do the foreigners wear only shorts and light tops, and the Balinese in this heat are wearing covered legs and arms?' she asked. Light tops? A blue tradie singlet each!

'The mysteries of foreign lands,' he replied, which was not any answer.

Would they ever find their way to Burma? Get the right visas? Withstand the rigours of yet unknown travels? Would they track down embassy staff there who could marry them? Both were carrying their birth certificates and their divorce papers. Was anything else needed?

Who was this woman Christy, anyway? A wild one, a rabid feminist, with some fem lovers more dramatic than even her. But a woman who counted him as unchallenged chief lover.

Without a doubt, they had both floated to Earth from another planet.

'How far is Mandalay?' he asked.

'Keep walking.' She turned and smiled, a weary walker's smile.

They caught up with another slower couple, and chatted a bit. French. The flags along the road— the "umbul"—were still standing from last week's Bali ceremonial day, they said.

Some shacks and thatched huts were appearing now, and kids ran across the track and a few pig and rooster noises were coming onto the street.

A boy approached them.

'Want room? Losmen? Cheap. I take you.'

'Talk to the ibu,' Ben had said.

They hadn't arrived into any proper village yet. They ignored the boy.

Now they passed a small and new tile-roofed restaurant, Resto Adit. Several family cottages on the main road were fenced with high stone walls and one Balinese ornamental gateway to each.

                BALI in its MIDDLE AGES

Other kids appeared, propositioning. So then they followed a girl down a side lane, past several shacks, and into a bamboo-fenced compound. Here were the chooks, the skinniest chooks ever seen, but noisy as they scattered.

The girl took them towards the larger shack. It had a thatched roof and only three external walls, and there were no other internal rooms. Kids scrambled around. The family bedding was one large raised platform under the roof cover.

The ibu came out to meet them. 'Want losmen?' she asked in broken English. 'I show.' A much older woman stood further back in the shadows.

Nearby stood several upended baskets with roosters underneath.

She led them to the smaller shack in the compound. The one small room held a narrow bed and a tiny table. Outside was a small veranda or deck, with another small, low table and two stools. The door appeared to have no working lock.

'Berapa?'

Ben.

'Four dollar,' she said.

From her apron, she pulled an old pad and scrawled a figure in rupiah.

He looked to Christy. They were tired, hot, dysfunctional.

'One?' he said.

'Satu?' She nodded.

Is it working? 'One night. OK,' he said to Ibu. He held up one finger.

'Ya,' she said.

Then, half-pointing, with her hand sloping down, she indicated a tiny shed, 'Weechee, weesee.'

Hmm, to an Aussie, it looked enough like a regular outhouse. He glanced at Christie.

Tomorrow would be another day, and they would survive.

'You're right,' breathed Christy. There's "WC" painted on the side, look.'

   BALI in its MIDDLE AGES

Next morning, two breakfasts arrived at their veranda, banana pancake and thick black coffee with grounds.

More north into the scattered village of Legian, they carried their packs. Again up a laneway, but better. Again solicited to look. Again a separate tiny bungalow, but better. Again with a promised breakfast, but with hot water for tea. Again a stuffed coconut fibre mattress, but wider. They had one weak electric light. And four stools all up.

Adjoining were two external rooms: in one a squat with ceramic food pads, and a water bucket, in the other a tiled floor and a tiled built-in water tub holding two feet of water.

'So I counted three eating huts we have passed that are close. We won't starve. We only need to be brave.'

'I'm not sure,' she said. 'They're small and rough. How do we know the food will be clean?'

'We came for adventure!'

They had passed also, far off left nearer the beach, a large new resort standing by itself across the grasslands. 'Legian Beach Hotel', their new ibu landlady said. 'Many dollar.' Her lips and teeth showed some red of the betel nut.

At Legian was one shop listing "TOUR". To Denpasar city, to Besakih's mountain temple, the monkey forest, art villages near Ubud, Uluwatu cliffs. They sold long-distance bus tickets to Lovina, Lombok, Mt Bromo and Jogjakarta and Jakarta in Java, along with a connecting car transport to the Ubung bus terminal near Denpasar.

'We saw a similar sign as we walked out of Kuta yesterday,' she said. 'Perhaps it was identical.'

'Yes, it looks like a same set of options. Do you imagine they each run their own tour trip?'

"Unlikely,' she said. 'My guess is they take the booking here, and the one driver collects us on the day.'

          BALI in its MIDDLE AGES

A car collected them at 7:30 and took them to an "office" on the Kuta's beach road. Transferred to a town delivery van fitted with bench seats for eight passengers, and handed each a bottle of water, they headed to Kintamani and the Tampak Siring springs, three hours away.

Three afternoons on, by now more familiar with Legian and the more major Kuta a manageable walk down the road, Jack and Christy stopped into their chosen place Warung Kadek for a drink.

Two European travellers were already sitting at the long bench.

'Hi,' said Christy.

'Hallo.'

'Where have you come from?'

The first was solid and his mate was skinny. Gunter and Jonn had been backpacking in Asia for three months.

Before their experiences could be mined, another young traveller, carrying only a traveller's shoulder bag, came into the hut wanting a drink.

'Aussie,' whispered Christy after a few words of the Fanta transaction. She asked the stranger if she'd like to join them. They became a brave party of five for some local dinner.

———

Terry:

'No, it isn't a mission,' I said. 'and it's not a hospital, either.'

'So OK, Terry,' said Jack, 'what is this place you work at?'

He took one more draw and passed me the lumpy rolled joint. Was offered it by a Balinese lad, he said. A sample, I guess.

We all sat on the veranda of the losmen room that Jack and Kristie were renting. Gunter and Johnny (the German lads), me and Kristie and Jack. We had talked on here for a couple of hours, and it was long, long past dark, and the evening was getting well-spent.

Jack rearranged me to sit at his feet, and I didn't resist. Kristie grinned at me like a conspirator, and all was mellow. Was I far enough away yet from my mission, my hospital? My prison of my own making?

He ran his fingers through my hair. Oh, yes. Yes please.

Shit, but I might have washed it this morning. Making new options deserves preparation.

The losmen deck with its twisted wooden handrails had no lights. The moon was still high, though, and that was the total of the light.

　　　　　　　BALI in its MIDDLE AGES

Kristie smiled at me. I think she was smiling. Then she looked at us both, me and Jack. She nodded. There was no mistake on that.

We all sat in the moonlight for a few minutes of silence, except for the chirping chikchuk.

She had been wedged between the two boys, and I saw her head drooping on and off down to Gunter's shoulder. Those three were several Bintangs along each.

Johnny stood up to stretch, and Gunter stirred too.

'We should go,' said Johnny. 'In the morning we are crossing to Java on the ferry.'

Kristie sat up and smiled at us once more, then shrugged. 'I'm off, too,' she said.

Is this what escape smells like? Only two of us remained.

As we made our way back in the moonlight to my villa at Legian Beach Hotel, I started answering more of his earlier question.

'I am a hundred kilometres southeast of Darwin. It's an Aboriginal cattle station, and it also runs a health clinic. I am the accredited nurse, and I have two Aboriginal partly-trained assistants. They are fabulous.'

'So, right, it's not an old-fashioned mission?'

'Oh, Jack, the old religious missions are past tense, they are a failed philosophy.'

'I would have to agree with that. They did no good service to the Aboriginal tribes. Another ignorant colonial oppression in disguise. In a religious habit.'

We turned towards the beach. A couple of places had Tilley lamps outside, hissing kerosene types.

'Tell me again, who owns the station?'

'The Aboriginal elders. The old English owner died being cared for by his native staff. He rewrote his will for them. He had no family himself.'

'I can't imagine it wasn't contested. In the courts.'

'They won,' I said. 'Before he died, he'd called down a Darwin lawyer to make his will as correct as possible. Never before was there anything like it. The old lot who now owned it then appointed an Irish bloke to run it for them.'

We were nearing my villa.

'Many medical cases?'

'Yes, we are always busy. Some cases are flown out by the Flying Doctor Service, but we cope ourselves where we can. I've done some urgent surgeries I wasn't supposed to.'

I thought a moment. Tell him? And what parts?

'Jack, I've quit. I'm not going back.'

'Why?'

'The station boss.'

He stayed silent.

'He cornered me once. He raped me. He's blackmailing me to stay silent. Hand in the till, is the threat.'

I unlocked my door and showed Jack in.

He left at dawn. 'I'll be back to find you after lunch,' he promised me.

'Bring Kristie?'

'Of course I will.' I had hoped for that answer.

But I won't be here after lunch today. By tonight, I'll be transiting through Singapore. There's no way I could tell him that, poor man, but I want no clues. He can remember me as Terry. I've been Terry for only one day, and a lot happened. Tomorrow I'll start with another name again.

My nursing assistant should have my Notice letter to hand over by about tomorrow, if my postal timing is correct. I'll be gone without trace.

I'll get up to start packing. What a total shame. I could have loved that man. Could have fallen for Kristie, too, I suspect.

But—

———

Christy:

Jack came in from the veranda. He didn't turn on the light, just walked up to the bed where I had crashed fifteen minutes earlier.

'Christy, you awake? I'm off now,' he whispered. He sat on the bed.

I leaned a little to him and put my hand on his arm. Help.

'Hmm,' was what came out.

Don't go. I don't feel OK about this. I need you.

'You sleep tight, and thank you,' he whispered. 'I love you.'

No … Can't you hear me? I'm frightened.

'I'll be back in the morning with love in my eyes and more mischief to be invented.'

He ruffled my hair in that way I can love. I don't understand what's happening. I'm not me? Not the me I know? Can I change my mind?

I think I drank too much beer.

I feel not strong right now. One arm is weak. It's not right.

We had so many plans for the next three months. Adventures to be created.

As we became used to this travel, we wanted to test being brave enough to spend some days apart. We would each explore what we could

                    BALI in its MIDDLE AGES

discover, and we would meet up again to continue on and share what we learned.

Eventually, we would find our way together even to Mandalay.

And then he was gone, and it became a very long night.

Long, long, long, until after dawn the door opened.

———

After a morning of tears and disillusionment, they locked up and headed out for the Legian Beach Hotel. Already it was mid-afternoon, and hot for walking.

They carried nothing, but they held hands with their fingers entwined, sure that that was not to Balinese street etiquette.

'I hope we are not too late,' said Christy. 'You said you promised after lunch. She might have gone out.' She squeezed his fingers.

'We arrive and we find out,' he said. 'We were busy, that's all.'

They turned into Gang Melasti and headed beachwards.

'How's that other arm?'

'OK for now. Don't think about it.'

Room 34.

'Something's odd.'

'Eh?'

'Terry's shoes and drying. Her other shoes. There's nothing here at all.'

The door was unlocked. There was no Terry. There was nothing. All was clean.

With his mouth open, he stood at the doorway, and re-checked the door number. 'It was 34, I'm positive.'

'Something is wrong, Jack. I don't know what. We should ask someone. What was her surname?'

'I, I, I don't know. She was Terry. I feel all stupid.'

They found the reception office.

'Room 34, a woman named Terry, but sorry, we don't know her other name.'

Room 34 had checked out today. The Balinese receptionist at the long marble counter looked uncomfortable, and would not give any more details.

'I agree with you, it's all odd.'

Along the main road, they made their way back and sat in the same Warung Kadek where the five had met only yesterday.

'She was wonderful and straightforward. We had fun. Now nothing makes sense.'

'Order me a coffee, one of those with the susu,' she said. That sweetened condensed milk. 'And I've peed my knickers a bit.' She had tears of fear in her eyes.

———

He never was more than a passable motorbike rider, but he did hold a current licence and had an international one with him—Ben again. The Ubud warung didn't ask anyway. For $2 in rupiah, they rented the bike for one day. No helmets.

'You know there are supposed to be some feral monkeys down at the bottom of our own road? It does have a second name of Monkey Forest Street.'

'But there's not much down south past the soccer ground. We were told that Sangeh was the good place to see the monkeys.'

Never in Australia had he carried a pillion passenger. Christy slung her leg around and gripped his waist. Their homestay had sketched them a simple map with the best way. Sangeh didn't look far direct, but the route was circuitous. Ubud and all towns in that part of Bali sat among the many rivers, ravines and ridges that formed the southern slope of Mount Batur. The roads were north-south, and the links between them were few.

The one sealed main road of Ubud gave way to dirt roads at Campuhan and thereafter. All the local drivers and riders, every bemo and bike, used their horn, a squeaky, shrill-sounding horn, again and again.

'Are they aggressive or angry?' she yelled to him.

'It's not different from Kuta,' he called back.

The roads were windy and narrow, and hid many a hole to be dodged. The few passing cars left little clearance.

He braked and slid.

'Hey?'

'I thought that pig would bolt across in front.' The pig had not flinched.

Every shack had chooks roaming about, skinny birds that would not give a decent feed. Those and their broods of chickens were a hazard all the trip.

The travelling was narrower now.

A whole waddle of geese, fifteen or so, were being shepherded along the track, and he waited until they could be persuaded to the side.

 BALI in its MIDDLE AGES

Exhausted, but not yet quite to Sangeh, he pulled into a warung on a rural corner. A traveller's place, not a village warung.

'Too much to chew?' she asked.

'Never.'

She grinned ever so sweetly. He was forgiven, he knew.

'Jeruk panas,' she said. He hadn't asked yet. Hot orange juice. It grows on one.

———

'OK, what now?'

They had crossed into Java by bus, taking the Gilimanuk vehicle ferry. On the Java roads, the bus driver was too reckless for their sanity, and they had asked to be unboarded early at Solo. Surakarta. Ben's yoga school once.

By walking the streets they found a guesthouse, a row of cottage rooms.

Over the ubiquitous morning pancake and black tea, they struck up a conversation in good enough English with an older man sitting out at the adjoining room.

'I travelling also,' he said. 'I go back to my village. I born in Bali, but now I live near Surabaya.'

'Do you have work there?' Jack asked.

'Ha,' said the man, 'if I have no work, I have no food, I die.'

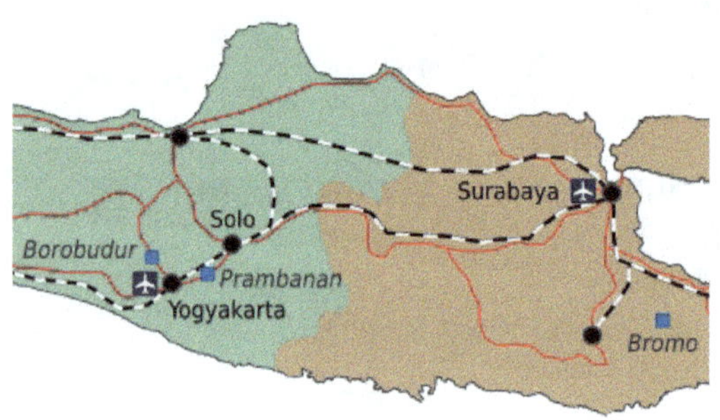

'The government cannot give you money for food if you have nothing?'

'In Indonesia, there is no government money like that.'

He paused, and he lit a clove cigarette, a **kretek**.

'I was a film-maker. For twenty years in Jakarta I have make information films about Indonesia. About many subjects. Many projects. Many people. These films I export to Holland. Many Belanda, the Holland people, lived in Indonesia before our independence. They left Indonesia.'

Therein, thought Jack, in those last three words, is a mighty chapter of world history.

'Many Belanda remember our culture and our language. Making Indonesian films for them was

          BALI in its MIDDLE AGES

good business. Especially on Bali. I make great money.'

'But now?'

'My customers in Holland no longer are interested. I make no money now. The old people all dying.'

'What do you do now?' she asked.

'Two years ago, I go back to this village near Surabaya, because my wife's family are there. I teach myself how to build a boat. Now I am a fisherman.'

After breakfast was over, Christy said, 'No dole. No pension. Create an income by any method possible, or face starvation. We in Australia have life too easy.'

———

From Jakarta, they flew to Tanjun Pinang on the tiny island of Bintan, ready to enter Singapore by sea.

But the imigrasi officer at the ferry terminal took exception to their passport and papers for no reason they could understand. No other Westerners were around. The afternoon was late, and he patently wanted to finish off his day without much effort. They could not board.

Possibly, however, for a different price it could be done.

Jack bristled. There wasn't going to be a "different price". But Indonesia has never worked on the indignation method. They retraced their steps into town to find some emergency sleeping place, and to try another imigrasi person and another Singapore ferry tomorrow.

That cost a lot more than any different price.

———

She was weeping.

'Explain it to me,' he said. He sat on the rumpled bed beside her.

'I don't know if I can. But something is very wrong. A lot of my left side is numb. No, it's not numb, I can feel my body. But it won't always move as I want. My arm refuses to lift far. Sometimes my fingers become useless.'

'Your leg?' One was shivering slightly.

'My left leg is OK most of the time. Most.'

She wept again.

'Jack, I've pissed myself several times. It happens and I can't control it.'

She paused.

'I'm so awful. It's all embarrassing, it's shameful.'

He held her a long while.

'Christy, we need help.'

'Yes, please.'

'Wait. I'll find where there is a doctor or a clinic, then get a rickshaw to take us.'

It was a small, cheap hotel, but the receptionist helped call a taxi, and the two reported straight into Singapore General Hospital.

Christy was admitted as a second-class patient. That implied one modest meal a day unless a friend visited with better. The ward was old and in poor condition. As much of his days as he could manage, he spent sitting with his mate.

Day after day, the cursory tests at the hospital were not revealing any clear diagnosis.

He did at least succeed in getting their Australian travel insurance office connected with the hospital accounts people. Getting the hospital to accept him as a correct person to report to if things got more difficult, he had won that also.

On the seventh day, the doctor advised that he couldn't identify the real problem. Christy was no worse, somewhat improved even, but she should go home to seek better medical treatment in Australia.

Couldn't identify? Wouldn't?

A three-month plan? No, they had journeyed four weeks.

After Indonesia? To Malaysia, Laos, Burma? No, no further than Singapore General Hospital.

Rebecca at the Disco

In that time of unreality, he was living in a nine-ton converted Leyland bus. After a long life as a metropolitan passenger bus in Sydney, it was now a habitable house-bus, with gas kitchen and oven and fridge, a bed and child bunks, even a shower and a library. He parked it and stayed in it on the hippie rural property of old mate Ben, out of Queanbeyan near Canberra.

But earlier in the year the bus had taken a "crew" of Jack, Christy and Jack's daughter Rebecca to an alternative lifestyles festival down on the Murray River, two lumbering days' drive southwards.

At an event that prized anarchy, using the bus as a kitchen and premises for a pop-up coffee shop was easy to pull off. Some of the revellers became regular daily clients and jolly friends. Coffee (and some oven scones) can do that.

The homeward bus trip carried two new friends, Deanna and Roberta. This pair, being on their own free-wheeling travel adventure, took the opportunity to get up to Canberra for free. The company was jovial.

The bus stayed parked at Christy's house in the Queanbeyan suburbs for the week after their return. Rebecca returned to her Mum's house, and he lived for the while with Christy. She was his partner those years, and staying over was normal. The visitors stayed with them that week, sleeping in the bus.

Christy didn't take long to intuit there was vibe in the air. 'Talk to me, Jack. Which one?'

'Yes, that's my problem. It's both of them. I could have fun with either one.'

She grinned. 'Ah, you have a problem,' she said, and went off to make a pot of tea, because it wasn't her having the problem, or not yet.

Christy worked at the local women's refuge. Late next afternoon she asked him again, 'Well, have you come to any decisions?'

'It's difficult,' he said. 'If I proposition one to some mischief, it would be flagrant on a knockback to then speak to the other.'

'Oh, dear, that's obvious. Sweetie, be brave.'

That evening, after they had all eaten, he found Deanna and Roberta together back out in the bus.

With both, he proposed the outrageous.

'Thank you,' said Deanna. The glances showed she was speaking for both. 'We need to think about. You are a crazy man. Give us time.'

They have thought about this, or something, already, he thought. I'm not crazy.

After work again next day, Christy came to him. 'Deanna and Roberta came to talk with me. Did I know what you had offered to them?'

'And—'

'So I said we had discussed it. That there aren't many secrets. That was close enough. And was I comfortable?'

'And your answer to that?'

'That yes I was comfortable. Part of the adventure of life. Like my own high jinks with Margie.'

Three nights later, the two women were ready, body, mind and soul, for the escapade. The three retired to the house-bus, drew the curtains and wondered how this went. Three awkward virgins.

'You OK?' was his first question with Christy on the morrow.

This was her last week at the refuge. College was to begin on Tuesday.

'Yes, I'm fine,' she said. 'My main problem is that I got so curious and envious that I wanted to peek in. I went outside to the bus, but you closed every

                    BALI in its MIDDLE AGES

curtain, dammit. What about you? Did you have a fun time?'

'We fumbled. We tried. No regrets all around I believe. Miracles? No. But pleased we launched ourselves into it. No one hurt and no one unhappy, but—'

'No one finding paradise? Need a hug?'

'Always.'

———

Deanna came to visit Jack at the house-bus on Ben's property several times over the following months. Each time, she caught the Greyhound bus from Melbourne.

Ben joked he rarely saw them. They slept late and talked always. Rebecca came out to the old farm and joined them for a weekend, and felt comfortable with Deanna. She had never been so easy around Christy.

After the dramatic scramble back from Singapore, and the medical tests following, Christy's health had been holding steady, although she knew difficulties lay ahead, despite all modern medicines.

He and Christy still considered themselves partners, although they had never claimed, very explicitly, any exclusive binding.

The mirage of that fairytale Mandalay wedding ritual was demolished decisively by now, but they were still mates, rather more sober about it and enjoying it for whatever it was.

Was Christy resentful?

'No,' he said. 'She's OK about knowing you are here.'

'Good,' Deanna said, 'I like Christy.'

To him that sounded too simple.

She picked up the toy beside the bed. 'Now, this thing I discovered yesterday. I had no idea. I imagine I can well entertain myself for the moment.'

Dismissed, he wandered off into the old farmhouse to yarn with Ben and Kerryn the girlfriend. A bedraggled and very bemused Deanna didn't surface from the bus for several hours.

'It's gone flat.'

Life could be like that. Ben saw it as a huge comedy.

———

'Jack,' she said on the next visit, 'I want to go to Java next month. A friend of mine is getting married.'

Deanna had lived a year in Jakarta as a teacher.

　　　　　　　　BALI in its MIDDLE AGES

'And I would be happy if you could come too.'

That took some negotiation. If he went, he would like to include Rebecca. He'd had his own plan to take Rebecca to Java and Bali sometime, but he was short on funds at the moment.

'I can lend it to you,' she said.

That looked an honest deal, because some contract payments were coming in soon and a loan would be returnable after that.

Again, 'What about Christy? She won't mind?'

'You're still anxious about me and Christy?'

'I know you are still that crazy man. But I don't want to break pieces of your life.'

He paused.

'Things with Christy are starting to diverge. I'm not all happy about it. But I haven't talked with anyone else about it before.'

'I'm sorry,' she said.

'You know how feisty and opinionated she can be. Well, last year I coached her on the mature-age entry exam for a degree course. She wanted more clout to her politics. More on reasoning and less on emotional argument. The past six months, she's been in college, you know that. And for academic essays, she's submitting raw polemic, unrestrained. So far, she's failed everything. It's "their" fault. Playing the academic game to get her ticket first is not on her radar, it's not her style.'

'Oh, poor thing.'

'She's getting angry with the world. And with me too. She's becoming a person I don't know.'

'Is that due to the MS? Or the worry about her future?'

'Quite likely involved in the mix. But I'm finding it stressful. I'm finding I become less wanting to spend time there.'

———

'One special thing I want to say, Becc,' he said. 'Last year in Central Australia, it was so challenging, right?'

'Sure was. Fun though.'

'Yes, it was fun. Well, Bali and Java are going to be more strange and challenging again. Everything in Indonesia is going to be different from how people like us live here. How people think and speak, how hot it can be, the food they eat, what the money is worth, how you buy things when there is no price written on them, what a taxi might look like, the sound of their music, stray dogs all over, cats that are not friendly in the slightest, dirt in the streets sometimes, smells. Everything you thought was normal about life will be "broken" there. And the people are so poor, so happy and so friendly. You won't ever be able to forget how different those things will be.'

——

The wedding was to be in Bandung, the groom and bride both having family there.

The Garuda flight was into Jakarta. Jakarta was home territory to Deanna, and more than one tuk-tuk or bicycle becak driver was taken aback at her confident street version of their 

language. Getting around was always easy.

'Something suitable for Rebecca to wear to the ceremony?'

'We didn't bring anything special. Bali had plenty of kids' clothes at the markets. It should be easy.'

It proved not so easy at all. 'We'll go to a regular department store,' decided Deanna. In the street, she called a tuk-tuk, that 3-wheeled tiny vehicle straight out of the latest James Bond.

The dress they managed to buy was bright yellow, to no fashion they recognised, but it did at least have some degree of formality to suit the occasion. It might get one day of wearing in its life.

———

Deanna shepherded them, all hungry, into a warung.

'Try the tamarind vegetable soup?' she said.

'I could.'

'What could I like?' asked Rebecca.

Something innocent. 'A salad with some peanut sauce? You can eat peanuts?' Her mother couldn't.

'I think so.'

Gado-gado.

It didn't work. She ate nothing.

She ate nothing all next day, merely drank a couple of soft drink.

He wasn't sure how to handle this. Rebecca can't not eat for a few weeks. He enticed. He offered samples. Deanna cajoled. But no food.

On day three, Rebecca came to him sobbing. 'Dad, I'm so hungry. I'm starving. Please help me find something I can eat.'

She was a growing kid now, but he hoisted her onto his lap.

'Hey, we can find some answers. You have to be brave and I have to try harder.'

The first answer was **soto ayam**, chicken soup. The Javanese most times made it mild, not spicy at all. Chicken soup was Rebecca's only food for a week, until she learned to cope with more.

'But be careful, Jack. Taste it for her first. Some cooks spice it up a bit, but most don't.'

All the trip, he pre-tasted everything for Rebecca. And Deanna tried to ask the kitchen each time to use no spices.

———

On the fourth day, the three visited Jakarta's prime memorial, the Independence Tower, the symbol of the "Pancasila", the five constitutional principles of the nation. This was Indonesia's heart.

The Pancasila was the lasting gift from Indonesia's independence pioneer, Sukarno. But Dr Sukarno had been exiled long, long ago by the military, and was never spoken of now.

'I didn't react or make any reference at the time,' said Deanna to him later. 'Did you notice anything when we were in the lift going up the tower, and the Javanese family were in the lift with us?'

'No.'

They were talking among themselves about Rebecca. "Gemuk", they were saying, and laughing. It was quite open.'

This Australian woman knew their language too well.

'Gemuk?'

They were all saying that the foreign girl is fat. They were repulsed and laughing, both.'

'Then they were repulsive,' he said. 'Rebecca is nine, and true she has put on a little pudginess in the past year, the sort that a year later can vanish as she grows. Please don't tell Becc. It's offensive.'

'The Javanese can be entitled and superior,' she said. 'Before colonial times, they were the rulers over a lot of what's now Indonesia, and then the Dutch were careful to leave them with their illusion of being the royals, and in control.'

'I don't care. They needn't be offensive. Don't tell Rebecca, please.'

———

The wedding? Deanna knew only the groom, who was all preoccupied with the ceremony. The three Australians were outsiders, uncomfortable, the interlopers in the party. Perhaps the invitation was not meant to be accepted. Or maybe bringing two more was culturally uncool, although he knew she had asked.

They sat and then stood to the back. Deanna made her polite congratulations at the file-past time and introduced her partner and his daughter —he was upgraded!

That wedding? They didn't discuss it much afterwards. It was left as a less-than-successful event. For four days hence, they booked a domestic flight to Denpasar.

———

'Jack, here is something we must try.'

They stood outside a small Bandung shop—all the shops were small—"Toko Jamu".

'OK? Yeah?'

Rebecca went to the door. 'It smells.'

'This is a traditional medicine shop,' said Deanna. 'They sell herbal mixtures for every possible health condition. Many villages have their jamu seller. We're going in.'

Rebecca declined the herbal shots, but Deanna chose two, for intelligence and good eyesight.

She spoke further with the apothecary, who had seated them each on a tall stool at his counter.

'And for you,' she said to Jack, 'they have a great jamu shot for special man strength.' She didn't translate further for Rebecca, but he reckoned Rebecca understood enough the meaning. Prudery had not been the custom of either her Mum or her Dad.

'Skol,' Deanna taunted.

The "man" jamu shot tasted dreadful, but it must have worked.

———

Jogjakarta: The Ramayana performance that Deanna so wanted to see. The thousand-year-old epic ballet of music and costumes and dance and not a spoken word—war and kidnapping and long forest journeys and returning at length to take the crown. It was a hero's voyage of testing, but scripted aeons before Joseph Campbell.

'Dad, they keep changing how to spell Jogja.'

"Good spotting,' said Deanna. 'Yogyakarta was the royal city, and they are allowed an exception. Instead of using the new spelling rules, they spell Jogja sometimes the old Dutch way.' Like most world languages except

BALI in its MIDDLE AGES

English, some national academy or department had straightened the Indo spelling and grammar.

They had taken the tour to Prambanan Temple, a mighty dark stone Hindu monument. After centuries of collapse, the stone had been widely raided for materials by the locals. Then after fifty years of restoration, it was still only half rebuilt.

From dusk and with lighting, this was the thrilling backdrop of their ballet that night. For four hours the production ran. Rebecca slept half of it.

'Overpowering. Three hours too long.'

Things one couldn't enjoy, but ought to enjoy, can still make big impressions that the memory can approve long later.

But it was time to fly out.

———

The Bali taxi driver took them past Kuta's Bemo Corner and west along Jalan Pantai to its end at the beach, and they got out to walk north along the beach. Past Gang Poppies.

Two proper backpacks and a "junior" one.

They found a tucked-away warung. There Rebecca—after daring to sample his mie goreng—discovered small green coconut-flavoured pancakes, the laklak. She would keep an eye out for those again.

Up a narrow alley called Gang Segara they found a losmen that suited. Considerable vacant land lay beyond there to the north, some coconuts, some other trees, and grazing cover for the cows.

Their place was neat with swept paths and luxuriant shrubs and trees. Two bamboo cages holding colourful and twittering birds hung on the branches.

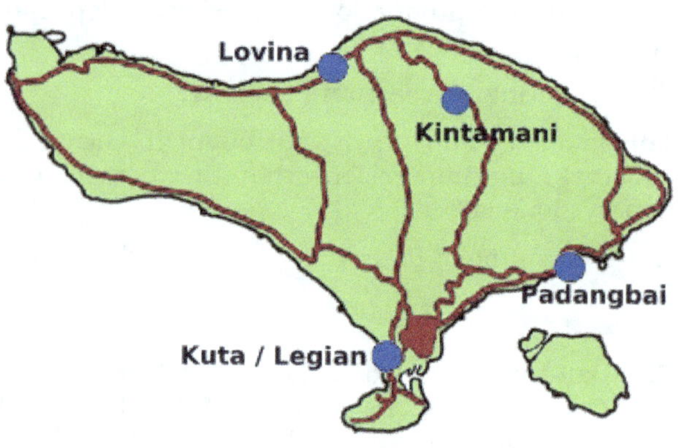

The ibu looked the travellers over, checked their passports—Rebecca's name was in his—and insisted they take two rooms for the three of them. No funnies in her rooms.

———

 BALI in its MIDDLE AGES

'Now,' said Deanna, 'do we go back and tackle Kuta Beach before the day is out, or leave it until tomorrow?' He and Deanna had each been on Kuta Beach before today.

'Tomorrow, D.' he said. 'I want to do some preparation first with Rebecca. How to handle the persistent sellers along the beach. I remember they were a bigger irritant there than what we have put up with so far.'

'Sure.'

'Also, warmer in the day may be better if one of us wants to accept an offer from one of the beach massage ladies. One of us at any time, and that gives Rebecca her option to say no, because I'm positive that's way too hard for her to try. One future day, maybe. For now, she's my cautious little girl.'

'Tomorrow I have another idea, too,' she said. 'We could go, all of us, to the disco dance night. I saw the notice back along the beach, where we passed the couple of compact hotels. Every Saturday and Tuesday.'

'Ha, and today is Monday.'

'Bingo. I suspect, though, that we might be early to arrive and earliest to leave.'

'Not your normal young nightclub customers, starting late, then drinking, bopping and raging till dawn?'

What else?

'No, but we can still have fun.'

How to do nightclubs, he didn't know. How was it said to his daughter? "Everything challenging."

He broke a lens on his spectacles next morning. Kuta had one Toko Optik, but its lab was across in Denpasar. In four hours and for $12, a new lens was made, fitted and shipped back to Kuta.

———

Deanna:

Tonight is the night.

Rebecca was uncertain about coming, but she's a good kid, and she took it on. She trusts her Dad.

'Hey Becc,' I said, 'I have some makeup with me. Let's fancy you up a bit. You used lipstick before?'

She blushed, I saw.

'Not supposed to have,' she admitted.

So I did her hair up and put makeup on her. By the time I was done, she looked older.

'Now, that dress we used in Bandung, get that out.'

Nine o'clock they let us in. No age restrictions here, as I expected, but she looked pretty smart and a bit grown-up anyway. She was chuffed.

Four others are here so far, two couples. One of them is entwined and bobbing already.

That's not counting the three young Balinese girls. "Staff" I must presume. One has danced with Rebecca for a while, staff duty, and that left Jack and me to dance a while. That was with the slower romantic tracks, too. Anne Murray, "Could I Have This Dance …"

Would the Bali girl be presuming any payment?

Funny, we haven't danced before. It takes some getting used to, dancing with a new partner. Not that I don't know this fellow. We work together well. There is so much we could do.

Yeah, tonight. It should be.

Another bloke and two girls have arrived. We might have a dance party yet.

This music now is not Bali music and not Java music. More dance music like home, thumping and base-y.

But Jack, hold me. Squeeze me. Make me feel hot.

Could I have this dance?

I have things I want to say to you. Close.

———

Last week, they had flown from Jogja to Denpasar, but today to go to Lombok they went by ferry. The large inter-island bus from Ubung bus terminal north of Denpasar would drive eastwards through Klungkung city first, then reach the coast after an hour. Jack and the two women had secured seats, but many later-boarding passengers stood in the aisles. Most had baskets or a bag or boxes, and before heading off the driver had lashed the bigger items to the bus roof. Their packs had gone on the roof. Further up in the aisle, chickens in baskets came aboard.

Everyone had been packed in, with the driver and his assistant calling more and more passengers aboard and helping push them tighter.

'Bigger than a bemo,' said Rebecca.

'But it's still the crowded farmyard,' said Deanna.

The music started up.

     BALI in its MIDDLE AGES

'Oh, yes,' called Deanna. That wasn't approval.

This was Western junior pop music, and in a shrill Indonesian style. It was loud and made conversation much harder. The noise continued the whole trip.

'Do we know how long?' she asked Deanna. He should have known, but this ferry trip was longer than the Java connection that he knew. He left it to Deanna.

'Do you recognise where we are yet?' she asked.

'No,' said Rebecca.

'This coast is near where we snorkelled a few days ago,' she said. 'We will pull into the harbour soon for our ferry. To Lombok should take a few hours on the water, possibly five. Then the bus takes us to Mataram. I don't know, forty-five minutes north in the bus. But it's Ampenan we want to get to, the old Dutch-era port town. So after the bus, a short bemo ride, I suppose."

She hadn't ever been to Lombok, she reminded him. Lived in Java a year, been to Bali a couple of times. But Lombok, no.

Down the long incline into Padangbai the vehicle queue was long and slow. Ahead of the bus, they could see one ship leaving. Another ferry had already moved into the next berth at the wharf.

The bus reached the control gate, and the port guard came aboard, talked with the bus driver, exchanged paperwork, and got everyone to file out and walk onwards while he counted the bodies. Only after the bus had driven on and had parked could they reboard it if they wished.

Two buses were boarding that ferry. Over a hundred passengers stood around to watch their buses ramped on. The ramp was scarcely wider than the width of the bus wheels, but the buses didn't hesitate, and moved at a steady pace up into the bowels of the boat. The ferry barely shuddered.

He lost track of Rebecca for a while, and was getting nervous, but she reappeared chewing a stick of sugar cane.

'I was hungry,' she said.

'Someone gave you that?'

'No, Dad, I bought it. Two.' She patted her pocket.

Pleased little villain. Learning some street skills.

They walked up the loading ramp after the bus, and Deanna shepherded them onto the open deck. Against the bulwark, she cornered them a sitting spot, a little protected.

'Now you can see why I said carry your jackets you've never needed, and some water and fruit, and sun-cream. Although there will be a couple of sellers wandering about before we sail.'

The Indonesian day might get hot, but it's not often clear-skied burning sunshine.

A couple of hours into the crossing, Deanna left for a while.

She returned all excited. 'Hey, come with me. The Captain has invited us to visit the wheelhouse, the bridge.'

And so they enjoyed kue and teh, tea and cake, with the Captain and his mate, on that Lombok ferry on that Tuesday afternoon. Deanna kept them entertained and laughing, while Jack and Rebecca looked at the wheel and the few instruments, smiled dutifully, and answered a little, in English, as needed.

His pocket instamatic snatched a portrait outside the wheelhouse door of the seamen and the two girls, their hair blowing in the wild sea breeze of the Lombok Straits.

———

It was getting dark when their bemo—they chartered it from the Mataram bus terminal—arrived into the Ampenan Port township. The short distance from Mataram, the small capital city, was all dirt road.

Deanna chatted with the driver, and he took them to a tiny hotel and waited to check they could get rooms. It was dark now, and there were no street lights.

In the daylight, Ampenan had a beachfront with a long old pier, and they found a few toko and a warung. There was scarce transport on offer, only two dokar waiting about near the jetty for business.

The **dokar** was a donkey cart or horse cart. A tiny horse, looking weary from the work, stayed harnessed to a two-wheeled passenger cart. A decorated roof fringed with tassels made the dokar cute.

'Like Ben Hur,' cried Rebecca.

'But with car wheels and car tyres,' said Deanna. 'Not in Ben Hur time.'

'Oh, yes.'

They went back, and Deanna spoke with Ardi, their desk man at the hotel. He beamed. He pulled out a sheet of paper and started making a map.

'In this street, you will find the Chinese Temple. You can go inside if there is no ceremony.' He sketched more. 'Along here is the Balinese village, and here ... the wartime administrasi.'

'Which way is this map?'

'Ah, pantai here. The beach. Our hotel disini. Here.'

'Thanks,' she said.

He scribbled more and pointed then to the Arab village and the Malay street. 'And here there are many Sulawesi people, and Dayak Kalimantan peoples are over here. Their homes are very interesting. They will talk with you.'

'So many?'

'Lombok people are the Sasak people, but in Ampenan so many traders have come from other places to live here. For many hundreds of years. Ampenan is the oldest town in Lombok. You should walk in all the kampong of our town. All of them are different.'

They left Ardi a happy man. It was a long and educating day.

By next morning, they decided to return to Mataram city for a few hours to look around. Deanna spoke with a dokar driver.

Jack helped Rebecca climb aboard from the rear, and he and Deanna clambered on following, and all sat on the sideways benches.

The springing on the vehicle was OK—or it was the pneumatic tyres—and the ride was bumpy but not unpleasant.

Should he wait? asked the driver in the Mataram main street, but Deanna dismissed him. She was competent to find a driver or even a bemo to get back to Ampenan.

———

Rebecca:

Dad went out to the money changer this morning. Deanna called me while he was out.

'Rebecca, I need to talk with you a while. Private.'

She's good to have around. Not quite like a big sister. Not quite like Mum either. Just good.

'I've been upset since last week,' she said.

Uh Oh, here it comes. I knew something was wrong. I knew it coming home from the nightclub. We didn't stay late, but something must have happened. Dad hasn't said anything.

　　　BALI in its MIDDLE AGES

I cried myself quietly to sleep that night. Something was unhappy.

'The nightclub night was special,' Deanna said. 'Your Dad is special. You know I've spent weeks at times staying with him in Queanbeyan.'

'Of course,' I said.

'Becc, I asked Jack while we were dancing together if I could move to Canberra and live with him.'

'Oh, wow,' I said. That would have been a bombshell.

'He thought about it a while, and then he said he's not ready for that just now.'

I put my arm around her, and I've never done that before. Hardly ever with Mum even.

'It was hard.'

I could see she was trying not to cry.

'But we are still friends. And you are too.'

She hugged me back. Shit, now it was me who started to cry.

'Your Dad will be back anytime. Becc, we have a fabulous holiday still happening for us. Lots of places to see and enjoy together. Let's go do it.'

Dad came back, and the subject was dropped.

I sobbed some more as I was trying to sleep that night. But it was also different.

Years ago, when Dad and Mum broke up, it was so hard to understand, so sad. I could never understand why it was happening. I was little. Still today I can't understand it, understand why.

But this week I know now that Dad is hurt too. Now that I know, I can see the tiny looks, the pauses, the silences that give him away.

I think it's 'cause I am older now, but I know he has to choose things in his life, and choosing things is hard. I find it hard. I'll be extra nice to him tomorrow. Without letting on.

There is another thing, too. This travelling around, going to new places. Now I can eat a couple of the foods, I'm getting used to it. It's getting exciting.

"It will be different," Dad said to me once. It sure is. All this Bali, all these places and their funny food and their houses and the rice-fields down all the volcano slopes and what to expect everywhere. Yes, it is so different. Well, it blows away the bus safari up to Darwin.

So, when I grow old enough, I want to travel too. I will see places. I could take Mum.

    BALI in its MIDDLE AGES

Deanna and a Sticky Trap

By a half year later, he was still living in his house-bus on Ben's property past Queanbeyan, taking in several consulting and specification-drafting jobs with the Department of Construction. In those years their brief included Canberra's water and sewerage network.

Jack had skills in designing the controls for filtration plant, for pumping stations, for under-city tunnels, and for radio-telemetry from the pipelines from the Cotter and Bendora dams. He had spent three years on their engineering staff previously, but was now freelancing.

That gave a lot of flexibility to travel, to become involved in festival planning, and to write occasional poetry—most of it now burned.

Deanna's loan was long repaid, and, having been jilted in Kuta, she had gone again to live in her "special" Jakarta. They mailed occasionally, cordial, sad, respectful.

Deanna had sound qualifications in teaching English, and, as before, finding work at a language school was easy.

Rebecca came out to Queanbeyan some weekends.

In Australia, it was a decadent, frugal, flexible, free life. And it was lonely.

———

She picked him up from his Qantas flight out of Sydney, and they took a taxi south, through the kampongs and slums that surrounded central Jakarta. He'd seen some of this here before, but this was more extensive and poverty-stricken than what he had known. The pervading smell was awful.

'How long did you stay in the family house? Your girlfriend's place here?'

'Oh, I'm still embarrassed about all that. Angry, to be honest. "Come and stay in my room," she told me. "We can make space, and you would be so welcome. It would be fun." I did think it would be fun, until—'

'Until?'

'"Stay longer, it's all good." So I stayed a month, but still hunting for my own place so Ayu could have her space back.'

'Then you found your current house?'

'So I announced I now had my new place. That's when the digs and innuendos started, from all the family. Obvious then. They had been

                    BALI in its MIDDLE AGES

uncomfortable and resentful I had stayed so long. There wasn't the honesty to tell me. All was fine, I had thought. I shudder now. I keep rethinking, how could I have so misjudged?'

'Sorry, Deanna,' he said.

'It's a thing here. I should have known. Always be pleasant and polite. No conflict or scenes.'

She paused.

'But—'

Further south, the suburbs became more genteel, and they arrived at the share house that Deanna now leased with a Javanese girl named Nrima.

At home, Deanna was polite and pleasant, but the old effervescence was not there, the smiles were more restrained. She had the evening meal prepared earlier, and the three of them sat to an early dinner.

———

They lay in the narrow bed together.

'It's good to see you again, to feel you,' she said. 'I missed you so terribly, especially early on.'

'I know. For me too. I wanted to meet you again.'

Desperately needed to meet her again.

'I made a great mistake in Bali,' he said. 'I want to ask you if we have another chance. It took me months to realise that, but if we have another opportunity to work together, I want to explore it.'

Where that might lead him he wasn't sure. Even to her Indonesia? What surrenders went into forging a relationship?

The light was still on in the room. She looked into his eyes; she said nothing for several minutes. He was dreading what might be the thoughts behind those eyes.

'It's too late, Jack. I loved you and I still love you, but also I have moved along with my life. Stay with me for the few days, and I can share my Jakarta with you.'

Lost.

'Or should I find some guesthouse or room nearby?'

'No, crazy man. We have never been as uncreative as that. That's a thing I loved.'

'Thanks, D.'

'Stay in my bed with me. But I don't want to have sex. That's getting complicated.'

'We can manage that.'

———

They found their way up to Ancol Water Park near the harbour area. It was Saturday, and Deanna had two days off. She had been smart enough to check they had swimmers. Ancol had a complete circular river of running water, whose hydraulics had him amused, but one area was a full surf wave generator, and that he had never seen or been in before. The crowds were heavy.

By the harbour they found a lunch. Approximately, they were comfortable together.

It kept coming back to him: "But—"

On the return taxi, she said to him, 'I know I said we wouldn't be getting sexual together, and you know you are still welcome in my bed.'

'Yes, I understand that.'

Sadly.

'But I want to make a suggestion. I have told Nrima some things about you over our months here. She's lonely too. She's quite lonely. Would you like to sleep with her some nights? You would find her lovable and gracious, and so grateful. Don't get her pregnant, sweetie. But I know, you've been snipped, so that's unlikely.'

He wasn't comfortable to take up that offer. Or rather, his disappointment over not winning any readmission into Deanna's future had left him saddened and that made him unwilling to take on the outlandish experiment.

'That's OK,' she said. 'It was "out there", wasn't it? I'll explain to her.'

'Thanks, tell her I can't do it.'

'Now, there are a couple more things to work out. Tomorrow, you must come with me to meet the neighbourhood headman. I must introduce you to him because you are living for the moment in his area. It's a traditional custom.'

'Sure. He'll imagine debauchery and immorality in your house?'

'No, I know him. It's normal and correct village etiquette.'

'OK.'

'The second thing. Did you hear scurrying inside in the dark last night?'

'I did.'

'Sorry to say, but it's a rat. We need to stop it. I'd like your help this afternoon buying a trap or some poison.'

He laughed. He had some purpose here after all.

Rat poison? 'That's the most abhorrent way. Where will it die?'

Rat trap? 'How can I extract a dead body?'

Sticky tray? 'Stuck but still alive? Yuk.'

They brought home a sticky tray.

In the depth of the night, a shrill scream rent the silence of the cottage. All three sleepers leapt out and turned on the lights to find two healthy rats ensnared with no chance in the glue pan.

'What do we do now?'

'We go back and try to sleep.'

The rat screams went for hours, getting feebler. But by morning there was still some life. It became his job, and the women wouldn't watch.

'I'm getting a snap-on-the-neck rat trap,' said Deanna.

———

With Merapi, he flew into Denpasar and found his way by taxi to Legian. Down one of the many lanes with the stone or concrete brick walls both sides, he found a losmen to suit him for his few days of decompression. Days of depression. Days of obsession.

The only water under life's bridge today was a fresh lot—yesterday's had passed to the sea.

Legian was looking more like Kuta since last he was here. More warungs—one called kafe: Indonesia uses a different sound for a 'c'. More accommodation, another resort along the beach, several more **kantor parawisata**, the tour offices. Why is it, across the wide world, that when a tourist lands into any interesting place, there are shopfronts offering transport or a holiday for a different place?

Kuta beach? No, he's not going near Kuta.

He planned a trip to Tanah Lot Temple, but didn't go.

He sat on Legian's beach for ages and wrote morbid poetry.

In the sand, he found one of those washed-ashore old Chinese coins with the square hole. Was it an omen?

He said yes to the massage woman along the beach, and had sand rubbed in with the oil.

Rebecca Hangs a Durian

He and Rebecca would play it differently this time into Bali, he determined. They would go to different areas, simple places, and explore different things.

Is that what happened? Yes, they did try a new way to look at Bali. But they would forget to do enough of the exciting adventures that make Bali, Bali.

'We can stay in a new area near the airport,' he explained, although Rebecca had no way to judge this decision. 'A resort at Jimbaran. We will be in a bungalow looking out onto the ocean.'

'OK.'

'And then a villa in the hills past Ubud, looking across the rice-fields.'

As once for Australia's Red Centre, and then for the Java–Bali–Lombok travels with Deanna, he again prepared a scrapbook for Rebecca with some sketches, maps and snipped pictures from travel agent booklets.

He had moved to Sydney a year back, and at the end of this weekend Rebecca with her scrapbook returned home on the bus to her bemused mother in Canberra.

———

1. This was the good life: Jimbaran Beach Resort.

So they would swim in the Indian Ocean outside their room.

They'd sit up at the bar and sip juices.

Try the pool.

Go back to their shiny-tiled terrace to get out of the sun.

Throw a balled-up sock at the gecko. 'Did you know the Balinese call it tragic bad luck if a gecko falls on you?'

They could open the pages of the one book each brought from home.

'I'm booking us a spot on the Uluwatu tourist bemo tomorrow.'

'Yes, please.'

'Spectacular big cliffs. I saw it once with Christy, but it was years ago, and I don't remember it much. We had seen a screening in a surfie bar in Kuta, on one of those old rolling film projectors. It

                    BALI in its MIDDLE AGES

was a short clip, and they played it again and again. I do remember its name though, a clip spliced out of *Morning of the Earth*. Famous. It was about Uluwatu and its cliffs and its surf and the Bali people there and the Aussies living there.'

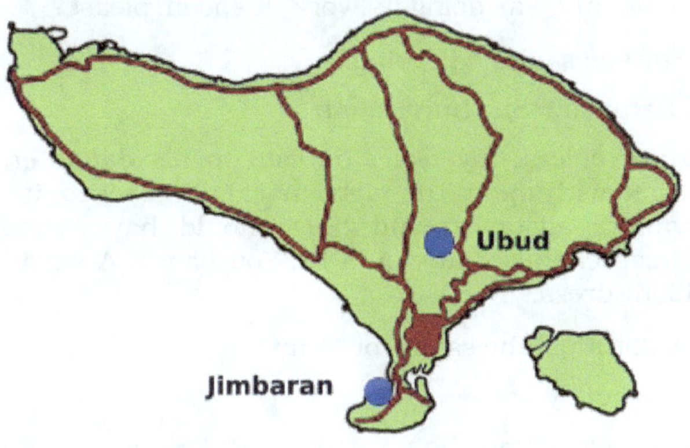

'Were they hippies?'

'You could say.'

'But different?'

'You could say. They were surfers.'

He went on. 'An enormous temple high up on the cliff above the beach and its surf. And a warung. Christy wasn't well. We couldn't get up or down the amazing cliff face. But I'm told they now have better steps to climb up and down.'

The lass from their bar by the beach arrived, with their two green young coconut. The tops had been carefully lopped off with a quick swing of a hatchet, and a delicate straw was propped into the juice. Kelapa muda.

'Dan sendok?' he asked. His tiny Collins dictionary was doing its work. A spoon, please?

'Ya,' she said, 'I will bring.'

Thank you. She hurried off.

'And tonight, my dear,' he said to his daughter, 'come with me to the night market. I checked, it's walking distance, and they should have some cheap clothes that would fit. You or me. A shirt? Light dress?'

'A sarong?' she said. 'For Mum.'

'Absolutely.'

Rebecca came home from market with two sarongs. He, after some whispered negotiation and persuasion, came home with the durian.

'Best,' said the seller-woman. Bagus. Banyak bagus.

The sarongs were "keepers". The durian, however, was banished from their room, and Rebecca tied it to the veranda post of the terrace.

After three days, the afternoon before they were to leave, the room cleaner—after the beds were straightened, the floors were swept and her duties were done—stopped beside him. 'Pak, I should take away the durian?'

He nodded. Do nods work the same way here?

The woman untied her prize for taking home.

———

2. Ubud. The brochure picture had been wonderful. The villa rooms of Cahaya Dewata were indeed superb. They were the only guests to tread those large halls and decks, to swim in the pool, to look over the expanse of steep, finely-furrowed rice paddies of the Ayung River ravine.

Rebecca took it bravely, but he knew that thus far it lacked the things any twelve-year-old bule appreciated.

'Dad, what's that sign supposed to mean? That one.' She pointed through the doorway.

'Oh, that.' The English wording was broken. 'No paper down that toilet. Not even toilet paper. Put the paper in that bucket.'

'Oh...'

"Their system can't cope.' He looked at her and smiled. 'Yeah. Hey, just get over it. Better than it used to be.'

The woman running the place, the only person they saw, described how to walk the breathtaking five hundred metres on the canyon edge uphill to the café on the road. The café did meals, whereas the villa supplied only the usual Bali breakfast. The café shared a similar view, and it became a daily second home.

'But, Pak,' said the woman, 'one night I can make you a big feast here. You pay me for the food from the market.'

'Becc,' he said up in the café, 'let's make some plans.'

'OK. We can do plans. We need plans.' She looked relieved.

Deanna could do good plans.

Plans:

☑ The in-house feast (probably for two)
☑ See the wild monkeys in town
☑ One evening, go to the theatre temple in town for the Monkey Dance performance
☑ Join a tour group to see Tanah Lot, the pointy-hat offshore temple that depends on the right tides to access
☑ Ask how we can find a track to walk down through the rice-field

Rebecca approved. It worked. And she had some photos to show her Mum.

The Island

Remember Berry Island? We know well by now the legend that islands can be romantic places.

Understand that Berry Island may once have been all surrounded by water, as good islands should be, but today Jack could simply step onto it He had walked from the Crows Nest Hotel on the Pacific Highway in inner Sydney, two kilometres down Shirley Road towards the Harbour, until the road finished. One more stride and he was onto Berry Island Reserve, and today the monthly jazz performance was in play.

Berry Island was a non-smoking premises. Aboriginal middens and ancient tool sites make it a treasured site to be protected from fires and damage.

These were the years when non-smoking by aggressive preference was novel, just starting to gain traction. "Nosmo", a new non-smokers' social club, didn't organise the jazz on that Saturday, but they were gathering at the jazz as an event on their own calendar. Nosmo sought out places—

and there weren't many—where the members could enjoy a smoke-free gathering.

He found his way to the Nosmo grouping, as he recognised a couple of recent friends, and he sat on the grass with the others. Several bidders vied to chat with him between the music pieces, taking their turns to talk.

'Can you speak any Indonesian?' asked Anne.

'A little. But you can?'

'From high school,' she said.

'Oh, I picked up a few words by being there.'

'Jack,' she said. 'I found this Balinese restaurant, a proper warung, in Manly Vale, and I've been planning to try it. Would you come with me next week? We can share notes.'

———

Anne:

About twenty-five years ago, when I was a girl, my father invested some money in a new copper mining company. Dad was a fitter and turner tradesman, so I don't know how he had spare money. Perhaps it was because we had owned our own house. They'd never needed any mortgage on it, because earlier he had won the NSW lottery, shared with a workmate, and the house was paid from that.

                    BALI in its MIDDLE AGES

Anyway, this copper mine struck gold, and the shares rocketed. Dad cashed in his windfall, and Mum and Dad decided to take me and my sister Dale on a cruise ship to Japan. I wasn't even a teenager. Our tiny, old ship was the Aramac, and this was its last trip before being scrapped.

Was this a dangerous trip on your tiny ship?

No. We even came through a typhoon on the return voyage, off Taiwan, but we survived that fine, and called in at Taiwan and the Philippines.

On the way up to Japan, we had a whole class of Japanese students who had been in Australia with their professor. I became their best friend. I adored them. They adopted me and taught me their language. I sang in Japanese with them on their final night concert before arrival.

Back at school, I wanted to study Japanese language. Something Asian. It was all so exotic, and not so far away in the world. But my new school, Cheltenham Girls High, taught only European languages. And Indonesian.

For three years Indonesian language became my favourite subject, my most successful subject.

For two of those years, I had a close friend Yvonne in my class and she lived two blocks from home. Her father was from Denpasar and her mother was Dutch. The house was always bubbling with people, talking, cooking satays, telling yarns, visitors arriving, hanging out. It was a very open house. My language skills blossomed, and that included some slang and street idiom. Our school teacher, Mrs Faulding, a gentle Quaker lady, frowned and frowned again at some of the ways I would use my words.

At the end of my School Certificate year in 1973, Mrs Faulding took her students on a trip to Indonesia, and I was one of the youngest to go.

We would be away for three weeks.

Did flights still refuel in Darwin in those years?

The experience was too big. That sounds like a detail that I no longer remember. But I can recall that the Garuda flight was awful. It was crowded and smelly. Some of the seats were broken, and couldn't remain upright. The lights didn't work, many of them. But the worst was the toilets. They were full, and not emptied, and they smelled. It was rather traumatic.

Mrs Faulding had arranged a bus to meet us at Jakarta Airport. Everywhere we went in Java and then in Bali, we went in that same bus. I remember it had a long banner along its side, "School Tour, Cheltenham Girls, Australia". All the locals knew we had come to town.

How did you find Jakarta?

Let's say Jakarta found us. It was busy and noisy and so hot. We were in a big hotel in the city, but lots of things were not working. And when we

　　　　　　　　BALI in its MIDDLE AGES

drove in our bus out of town, Jakarta was so big and so poor and stinky. So many slums and humpies. It was all overwhelming for Aussie schoolkids.

We spent one night I remember in Bogor. It was cooler, and Mrs Faulding took us to the Botanical Gardens. They're supposed to be famous, but it was rather boring. We went up over the mountains, across Puncak Pass.

Bandung?

I think so. Can't quite remember.

No, sorry, I do remember Bandung. It was New Year's Eve. We were in the local movie theatre watching a movie with Indonesian subtitles. We all sat in one long row. Then in came as many Indonesian boys and they sat straight in front of us.

The middle of Java was not tourist central in those years. A group of European girls was an irregular event for Bandung. Some of the girls were blond, and that was never seen there. The lads were uncontrollable, curious, wanted to stroke the hairs on the arms of the teenage girls. Indonesians had smooth, hairless skin.

We survived.

But at Yogyakarta we stayed longer. I was housed with Heidi Faulding, our teacher's daughter, who had also come. I guess I was treated as the youngster in the student group.

I did like the Buddhist temple at Yogya. We stayed for hours. Have you been to Borobudur Temple?

Funny you ask that one. No, I haven't. I have been to Jogja twice over the years, but long after you were there. Both those times I went to Prambanan, the other big temple, the Hindu one. But never Borobudur. Not yet.

Not yet. One day? So you have seen those other places in Java, too?

Yes. We worked our way along by bus once to Jogjakarta. Then I've been back northwards by overnight train another time. We stayed up into the night, watching everything from the train. When it got into the jungle hills, we passed so many tiny villages each with one public electric light, and the villagers would be all gathered outside around the one TV set.

Oh, wow!

Memories. Well, after Yogya, I remember we stayed a night at Tretes near Surabaya. It was cool there, and I was feeling sick, so the cool helped. Traveller sick, belly sick. Another girl even went to Surabaya Hospital to be checked. The others had a look at Surabaya and we moved on to Mt Bromo, and they walked up at 3 am to a sunrise, and again I wasn't well enough.

          BALI in its MIDDLE AGES

Then we were in Bali.

Over on the ferry?

It's lost. I don't remember. I suppose so, because we still had our bus.

We were in a hotel in Denpasar, Like Jakarta, some things were short on maintenance. We had squat toilets, but we had become used to them by now, them and the water tubs and scoopers, the gayung. *We lived in our Denpasar hotel, but each day we went off in our bus somewhere.*

Hey, we are both all finished, and the night is getting late. I do need to be up early. Can we meet later to talk more about Bali?

———

Anne's dinner next week was at home.

'Well, now, that complicates us a bit, doesn't it?' she said later.

'Hmmm,' he replied.

'There's one other important thing I haven't talked about with you yet. Next month, I'm going to Europe with Katherine for nine weeks.'

He sat up.

———

At the airport three months later, he waited for her arrival from London. He hadn't told her. Communication to a far traveller was not easy.

She saw him far across the arrivals hall and broke into a sprint along the hall to leap upon him.

'Jack,' she said when she could speak coherently, 'come back over here and meet my parents.'

He had never met them before, and they were bewildered.

                    BALI in its MIDDLE AGES

Anne with No Backpack

'**B**ut I have a problem carrying a heavy backpack,' she said.

Travel in Australia by car had not been a problem in their first handful of years together. Broken Hill, the outback mining town. Flinders Ranges in South Australia. Then up through Coober Pedy opal country, Ayers Rock and the Alice, tropical Darwin, the Kimberley, Broome's Cable Beach. All in a sedan car and a 4-peg/1-pole safari tent.

But the subject kept reappearing. What about Bali?

'Back when I was around Europe with Katherine, my backpack was an issue. I bought a different one over there to try a more comfortable fit.'

Anne had structural problems with her back, had always had since her teenage years, and for most things she managed fine enough. But when travelling, the weight on her back was difficult.

'I'll make you a deal. Something small and light you could manage? But not a serious pack?'

She nodded.

'I saw what you struggled home from the UK with. I've seen what stuff you do a car trip with. Plenty!'

She grinned.

'Here is a deal. We can take a single backpack and I'll carry it all the way. But then I get to choose every item we carry. Every item I carry.'

An anxious week followed where he sketched out what items were on the allowed list:

☑ Three sets of knickers each
☑ Three lightest tops
☑ One trousers
☑ One shorts
☑ No towels
☑ Toothbrush and shared shampoo

It was a little more than that savage list, but not a lot more. By week's end, she had surrendered, but it was not how she had ever known how to pack for travel.

'Show you how to "do Bali?" I can do that,' he bragged. 'There is only one climate, hot, so no cold weather clothes. And one good way to eat the food —food stalls selling honest Indonesian food.'

'Dale got so sick in Sanur,' she said, 'and we were careful, we ate only in our hotel, good food like at home.'

But the deal was still struck, and only one backpack went to Bali.

———

　　　　　　　　　　BALI in its MIDDLE AGES

They arrived with no bookings.

On the last trip, with Rebecca, he had booked everything before leaving home. The tourist office had organised the places for him along with the Garuda tickets.

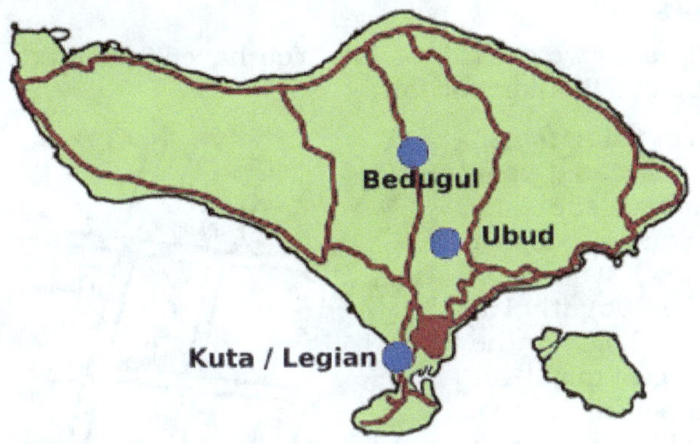

This time he vowed to go back to the old way he knew, find places as needed. Bargain. If necessary, play off a couple of places, quote the other's best offer.

The airport taxi let them out in the middle of Legian on Legian Road. In the main street, they sat at a warung and he ordered two kopi susu. Local black coffee was too rough, at least until they might acclimatise.

With their bags they were obvious. One man walked across the road and asked if they needed a room. No, thank you.

'Do you remember?' she prompted.

But no, he wasn't recognising much of his old Legian. For fourteen years he hadn't been in Legian.

'I guess we can't draw lots. You haven't done this before. Wouldn't be fair.'

'I'm going to call this as your party,' she said. 'You boasted how it's done. Go do it. I'm minding the bags. I might get a soft drink, too, while you run off and then come back with your best find.'

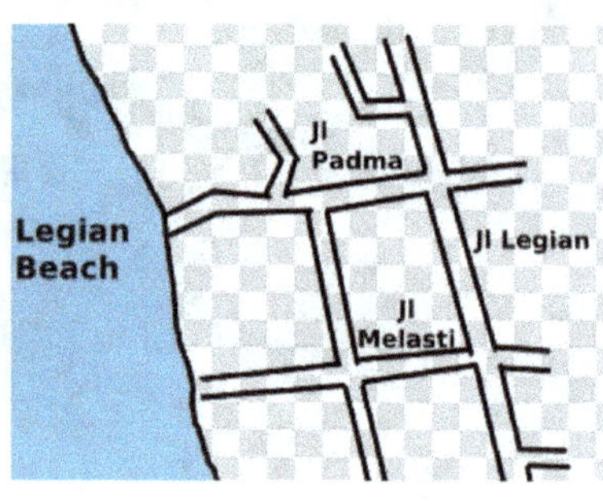

He walked north, ignored the old hotel on the other side, then took the first narrow road going towards the beach, and down past Warung Happy on the left.

Walking without bags doesn't attract the attention. Why did the touts offering "losmen?" or "want room?" annoy him so?

BALI in its MIDDLE AGES

Several discreet signs, hand-painted as always, did offer "losmen". Most were family compounds, behind stonework fences, and difficult to assess from the road without entering and starting to negotiate.

All the shacks and cottages here were recent, and last time this had been open land. The road now had property frontages right along, and countless narrow lanes with high walls. He passed another small eating shack, a wooden bench facing the street, all dark and suspicious, but he was not going to describe it in those words to Anne.

Nearer the beach, and he had come perhaps 500 metres, were a small store, what in modern words would be a convenience store, stocking a few foods and daily goods, and two more obvious accommodation places, with name boards. He walked into the first, was shown by the ibu the one vacant room of the three there, got a price, got a lesser price, and promised to return. "Thirty minutes," she had allowed.

'$10 a night,' he said.

'Is it any good?'

'It's great. Come with me. It's only ten minutes away. The bed is fine, and it has mosquito netting. We get breakfast included.'

'I should think so.'

'There is a room fan, and the usual foot-stand dunny, but— And it's only a hundred metres from the beach.'

It became a six-day stay. Bungalow Nyoman was where Anne, the traveller this time without a case, without a backpack, settled into the hippie and minimalist version of "doing Bali".

———

Next week they checked into the Ashram Hotel at the edge of Lake Bratan at Bedugul.

It was a project built to give training to unemployed people, he had heard, and that may have been true. But it was a quaint place. The brick support pillars at the front made him think of what Australians would label California Bungalow.

The facilities were minimal, not including any way of boiling any water, no breakfast, and it had the too-familiar stuffed mattress. Their room had a musty smell. The rate was cheap.

'A bit run down,' she said.

But the view north across the lake was stunning, and they were in close walking distance to their targets, the lake and the Botanical Gardens.

They would see their intended places, and leave. Two nights, then get out.

In the morning, Anne found a thatched stall nearby that had some fruit and bottled drinks, so that made a breakfast.

Then, not three hundred metres leftwards around the lake they found the boatmen. It was the boat ride across the lake and back that they wanted. Stumbling, and in English, Anne negotiated for a price, a time length and a planned route on the lake. The man would row them.

She called back his price in Indonesian. She surprised herself, but our boatman, whom they soon came to know as Sjam, heard it.

'Apakah berbicara Bahasa Indonesia?'

'Ya. Saya bicara. Sedikit,' she answered. Yes, but only some.

She braced herself now. Sjam wanted to speak Bahasa with her from now on, dropping to English only when he knew Jack wanted to understand. Jack understood only the few Indo words from long ago. Anne's schoolday language won handsomely over his desultory adult learning.

She started haltingly, but soon was chatting along in Indonesian.

'See over there,' said Sjam when they were half across. He pointed along the eastern lakeshore. 'Lihat gua?' he asked. Those caves?

'Melihat?' he asked again.

Jack looked to Anne.

'You should see some caves there, he says.'

'OK, I can see a couple.'

Sjam told them these were the "Japan Caves".

Japanese?

Some stranded Japanese troops were hiding in there late in the war. They held out there for some time.

Sjam said his grandfather was one of several Balinese farmers who were forced by the Japanese to dig out the caves. He and the others were shot after the job was complete.

For a while, they sat in silence, as Sjam rowed a large circle swinging north.

As he came back towards their starting spot, there was a cleared area on the western shore.

'A large resort is to be built there,' said Sjam.

'Apakah itu bagus?' asked Anne. Do you like that plan?

She was leaving her judgement unstated? Waiting to hear Sjam's answer first? He was following a few words.

'It is not good. Our village does not want any resort here.'

'It makes you sad?'

'Sedih. Sangat sedih.' Very. It's bad.

Their shoes came off, to wade through the lake water, and they paid their friend Sjam a good tip.

'You said you wouldn't remember.'

'Well, it came back.' She smiled.

They headed off to the Botanical Gardens, two kilometres into Candikuning. The gardens were reputed to have a great rose exhibit.

His father came from Ballarat in mid-Victoria, and the climate is cold in winter there. Ballarat prided itself on its roses, so he had always believed rose climate was cold climate. So how did an equatorial, steamy country grow roses? That was the afternoon's adventure.

After finding more orchids there than roses, they left the gardens. At a roadside stall they stopped for a snack, settled for a **pisang goreng**, the deep-fried banana, then negotiated a driver for tomorrow to Ubud.

At Ubud, at the main road, not far from the old and dilapidated two-storey market building, they asked to be let out.

'You ever tried frogs' legs?' They stood outside a choice of two eating spots.

'Yes, in Denpasar in 1973. The next answer is no.'

'What about a hot orange juice?'

'OJ, hot? No, never. OJ should be cold.'

'Trust me.'

'OK.' So in they went and he ordered.

'Not sure about this,' she said between sips. But she drank it. 'I'll think about it.'

'That palace across the road, I heard it takes travellers. It has rooms. Otherwise, we can head down Monkey Forest Road around the corner.'

'A palace? That place? Then why don't we try. I'll try. Me a princess? Stay here with our stuff for once.'

She looked at him. She still held in both hands the empty glass, and her hands had a gentle tremble. He had watched it before. He said nothing.

'And thank you for being my porter.' She smiled and left.

In ten minutes, Anne returned, smug. 'We're in. $14. I took it. Three nights. That bungalow we can see over the wall, the one in the very corner. The other two had people already.'

He hoisted his backpack to cross the road.

The bungalow was ordinary. Ordinary with a big "O". This wasn't the royalty's quarter. But they stayed their full seven nights of Ubud. Moving on when a spot is good enough makes no sense.

Bombs

Rebecca called on his cdma flip phone. For two years so far, they had been caravanning Oz, and were now on the Western Australia coast.

He had always refused to have one of those earlier brick-sized portable phones for work. Someone would want to call him. The day he retired he bought a new small model for himself.

'Dad, you've heard the Bali news?'

'The bombs and the hundreds dead? Yes. Awful.'

'Dad, I'm assigned to the support team.'

'You heading straight into Bali?'

'No, I'll be in Australia. Lots of the injured are being flown to Darwin and Perth for medical care. I might be in those places sometimes. But I'll be working from Canberra for starters.'

His girl was growing up. Her Mum died last year, and now she's forging her own future.

'You take care. I love you.'

—— —— ——

Two years further along, and they were still caravanning, of "no fixed address". This was the Darwin Dry.

It was dinner at the Sea Dogs Italian Restaurant at Cullen Bay, a birthday celebration with Veronica and John. John was CEO of the Tiwi Islands Land Council.

'Jack, that's your phone,' called Anne over the noise.

The mini cdma phone, battered by now but still working, was ringing, hanging in his bag over the chair.

"Rebecca," it read.

'Dad, it's me.'

'Hello, my dear, what's up?'

A phone call from the Solomon Islands was quite irregular. Rebecca was working there on a two-year posting with the international peacekeeping team.

'Dad, I'm OK.'

'Good. You're OK?'

'Dad, A lot of us got caught up in the street riots in Honiara today.'

Pulling Anne close, he pressed the phone into loud mode.

'Say that again.'

'The riots here. You haven't heard yet? You will. I needed to call you to tell you I'm safe. I was afraid you would hear it on the news first and be worried. Some people have died, but we managed to escape back into our compound. For the moment we are locked in, but we are OK.'

In two weeks, she was due for home leave. He knew that.

'I want to see you, Dad. Will you still be in Darwin if I land into there?'

'I'll be here, bet on it. We'll be waiting.'

'We'll be still here, Rebecca. We can stretch out your Dad's birthday, and all sit with champagne by the sunsets at Fanny Bay.'

Anne had a four-month job at Darwin Health, and they would not be taking the caravan south until the wet season was threatening, late October.

Yes, Becc, they'd be waiting.

East Coast

'**J**ack, I need to stop moving around. I'd like a home, a place to live, a community where I belong.'

For six years now they had been travelling around Australia. Desert, tropics, seaside, mountains, winter (go north), summer (go south), west, east, Red Centre, the Nullarbor, the Kimberley, snowfields, all except Tasmania. But those travels are a whole 'nother story, a different log.

Everywhere, the heavy laptop went with them, chargers and disk drives fitted around, and the tiny cdma phone that he had converted to a squawking slow modem. Software work and occasional connection back to Sydney earned valuable travel dollars.

But now it was time to stop and do different things. They returned to the home in Sydney. House rental had been most of the income for their frugal travelling, and with the pieces of work along the way, they had broken even. Now they smartened up that house and sold it.

The new home was in Queensland, a townhouse by the beach in a regional city. So then for several years it was time for settling and enjoying and living contentedly. And earning a few dollars.

But surely as day after night, the travel bug must return.

Wifi had appeared, and so had the miraculous tiny Asus-eee computer, the first netbook. Its minimal memory supported Linux software but was too limited for Windows. Asus did squeeze a Windows onto one version, but it was so hobbled as to be nearly useless. However, the masses recognised only Windows, and the Asus experiment, trying to invent a practical new computer category, slowly failed and stopped selling. But Jack was a software man. He bought the tiny eee on its release day, reshaped its Linux to suit travelling, and used it for trips for the next ten years.

The sale of the caravanning rig left money sitting in their pocket. A windfall expedition around the Mediterranean countries happily emptied that pocket, but that is yet one more different travel log.

Same skills, though. Cheap fares. Selected two-star places, often found on the fly. Don't carry too much. Eat local. Experiment. Make friends. And see the maximum.

                    BALI in its MIDDLE AGES

Ah, but there were two new travel tricks by now. Besides the eee PC with its wifi, there were the two-wheeled fabric trolley bags to do away with that backpack weight. A Rebecca discovery. Anne had now wandered the Mediterranean, managing with her own new properly-sized luggage bag.

'Everyone else wants four-wheelers.'

'Nah, for the real traveller, that's the wrong answer. Those only work across the departure hall.'

Eventually, back to Bali?

But was it safe to travel? Safe in particular to Bali? Two terrorist bombing catastrophes had struck Bali and its burgeoning visitor industry. What cells of plotters remained to inflict another round of hate and havoc? Osama bin Laden was dead. Was that a new factor?

Surely it was now safe?

———

Jack and Anne and the eee went out of the Gold Coast Airport and to Kuala Lumpur. Cheap airline Air Asia had their hub in KL, and it flew back east to Bali at much lower overall price than anything direct to Bali. It should be a dollar-saving strategy, but it was nuts.

They paid a driver from the Bali Airport, a process now orderly and price-controlled, and they were delivered straight to Sri Bungalows in Monkey Forest Road. It boasted a pool and air-conditioning. The booking was for two days, done online from home. At $60 a night, it was a star above their regular price bracket.

'We will wing it from there.'

'No, never,' had said various friends.

After several years, and after moving to live in a new place, one's friends become a fresh lot!

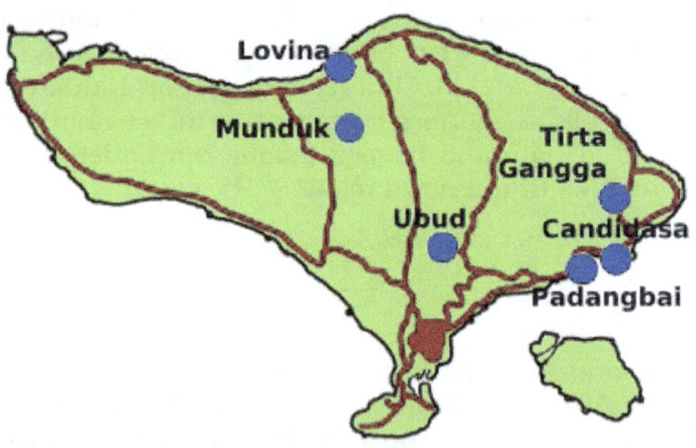

'We would never travel without all the transport and all the night stays secured. How could you live with the uncertainty about finding a place?

                    BALI in its MIDDLE AGES

You might get stranded with nowhere to sleep. How can you know what a place should be worth? Do you spend all day inspecting places and bargaining? Never!'

But they did invent it all from there, around all the east coast. It was the way they knew. Nowhere else on that trip cost over $40, and no village presented any lodging effort beyond walking 500 metres, and making a pick, and going in to ask and look.

'There's been a moral in all that,' he said a week later, lying on a beach.

'Yep. Book one first night for arrival. Book nothing else.'

'Have we tried that in peak season?'

'When is peak season? We arrive when it suits us, in our life. In the Wet or in the Dry.'

'Wonder if one future day we get caught out?'

'Don't care,' she said.

Ubud's Jalan Monkey Forest was these years built all along, down to the animal sanctuary at the bottom end. Most of the rooms were in bungalow form, and long, lush Bali walkways led to each bungalow and on to more bungalows. At the end of the rooms, the land behind was paddy fields of rice. Their own bungalow was the last one, and their terrace looked straight across the rice.

The restaurants along the road also looked out at their rear to the same rice-fields. A glass of fresh lime juice, a nasi ayam, and a layered jelly dessert, that hard-to-find kue lapis. Oh, and two Bintang.

After their two nights at Sri Bungalows, they walked three places downhill and checked into the Warsa Gardens. This was down to their regular stars rating now: this place had no uniformed full-time doorman to welcome and carry bags. The bungalow still looked on the same rice-fields.

Massage girls (and a few boys) spruiked on the streets, some early in the day, but more after

                    BALI in its MIDDLE AGES

dark. They both signed up. Two by Balinese massage, please, total $14.

'Hmm,' Anne said. 'Not what I'm used to.'

In a side lane, she found a Thai massage studio owned by a European woman, who had trained Bali masseurs in the Thai method. Before the trip was over, Anne had enjoyed eight massages, and the Thai place, Shangri-La, in that lane off Monkey Forest Road, she pronounced her clear favourite. At $14 a time.

He wandered into a DVD shop between Monkey Forest and Hanoman, above the soccer field. In their last time in Bali, in those days before the bombings, he had bought a couple of DVDs. One worked, the other was junk, but the price was unbeatable.

This whole shop was dedicated to racks of DVD titles, movies, TV series, even software. $1 a disk. $15 for a hundred disks. It was wrong, surely. Bootleg, contraband, piracy, call it whatever, but it had to be wrong. He filled his basket with $15 worth, practising his rationalisations. With Rebecca at home he could have a party.

———

Last year, he had pierced his ears, and he was defiant in his stainless steel rings. "For you to guess. And you'll be wrong."

Did such a style, because he liked the style, exist in gold? For a gold price. A Bali gold price that might be more affordable? It was not a pressing priority, but it was easy to ask.

The jewellery agent outlets now appearing in Ubud they ignored.

'Rebecca and I went to the workshops in Mas and Celuk,' he said. The minibus tours would drop us in the showrooms there for an hour at a time. We would be en route to some other destination, but they wanted their margin from any showroom sales to their bus passengers. We were rarely buying customers in those days, but it was interesting watching the items being made. Our drivers watched us with hawk eyes, to be sure they got their percent.'

It was obvious that his long-practised method of finding a driver by just waiting and bargaining on the street was no longer working well for Ubud. The new drivers' cooperative was on a corner along Hanoman Road. The coop shack looked as though it was once a warung, and several men hung around day and night. The car price to all Bali destinations was whatever the coop listed.

So they took a coop car to a gold showroom in Celuk. Nothing resembled his captive-ball rings. Lightweight questions to the showroom attendants returned scant knowledge of designing like that in Bali. Is gold too soft to keep a ball clipped with no risk?

He was discouraged. They retired a while to a coffee corner.

'Ever tried that "Luwak" special coffee?'

'Coffee beans re-shat whole by the civet cats? No.'

But they bought one packet of beans, expensive, to take home for a brave later day.

For tomorrow they had decided to move to the ferry port of Padangbai, and then later to Candidasa. He was sure he had snorkelled once somewhere along that coast, and he had enjoyed the different Bali in the towns that far along the southeast. He signed a driver from the coop to take them to Padangbai at the standard rate of 350,000 rupiah. They would do a run around the whole east coast.

———

At a car park near a boat jetty they were let out, and at Wait Kafe on the park corner, they sat to drink teh, and plan. Plan became stow bags at the café back wall, explore together.

Along the beachfront were several accommodations, with dining and pools, and several diving academies with certification tanks. Padangbai had its own diving boats and was also a fast-boat connection to the Gili Islands with even better diving.

They trudged uphill and accepted a room instead at Serangan Inn II. No pool. Breakfast but no restaurant.

So, up there, what was the good side? 1. The view. 2. The view. The room was fine, and foods were available close by. The town beach lined with fishing and tourist boats was three hundred metres away. Their centre room upstairs had a postcard view across Padangbai including all the wharf on the right. And all wider than a regular photo shot. Perfect.

Then a few days at Dewa Bharata Bungalows at Candidasa, facing straight to the beach. Idyllic? Lazy?

'Well, we have had more successful stays than here,' she said, as in turn they departed

Candidasa. He'd been unwell. It had not been idyllic.

'Agreed. But it's again time to move on.'

They had weakened: they had a booking. She had managed last night to find some wifi and booked a night alongside the Tirta Gangga Water Garden.

With Deanna and Rebecca, he had once been to Tirta Gangga. It was then a fresh and ironic ruin of a water temple, and it was a side stop on their trip to go snorkelling on the coral.

Built by the local king after the Japanese had pulled out, the water-garden was soon then demolished by the great volcano Agung blasting across Bali. But now it was reported as all renovated.

Their place was the Puri Sawah, the "Castle in the Rice-fields", pleasant and genteel rural Bali accommodation, at $25. It was indeed exactly alongside the gardens. The air was cooler, and no air-conditioning was needed up here.

'A long amble through the Bali fairyland, and a rice-fields trek before sunset,' he said.

———

'I have been to Lovina before, too,' he said to Anne, 'but I don't remember much of that. We didn't look properly.'

'With Rebecca again?'

'Yes, and Deanna.'

Just one night they had stayed in Lovina, he said. They had been en route to Singaraja nearby, the old Dutch-era capital. Deanna had wanted to see Singaraja's old buildings and the famed Chinese Temple.

With the two women, he had arrived into Lovina on a small tourist bus, a Perama. Then they had found a car to travel a short distance along the main road, until they spotted a couple of villas and they were let out to arrange a room.

Before that day was done, the three of them had managed one short walk to the Lovina beach, a

                    BALI in its MIDDLE AGES

beach they thought held little great appeal. So next morning they travelled on again the thirty minutes to Singaraja. Singaraja in its turn, they had decided, was old colonial, a non-tourist place, not courting the visitor.

The driver broke into Jack's story. 'Where is your hotel in Lovina? Where I leave you?'

'Complicated,' he said to Anne. 'Explain to him that we don't know. Let us out at whatever is central Lovina.' Sometimes using Bahasa is easier.

On that long-ago Lovina visit, he thought some more. They had discovered that day an old temple fenced in stone. The fence had quite violent mythical cameos carved in it, and he remembered shepherding his daughter away.

The drive took three hours.

'Disini Kalibukbuk,' said the driver. 'We at Kalibukbuk. Best place.' They were at a junction on the main road.

'This is Lovina?'

'Yes, Lovina. You walk that way, ke sana, you find room. Good bungalow.' This was a long way from his home corner of Bali.

Beside the road, they stood out their trolleys, and they paid him. This time, they would make Lovina work.

Down the winding road to the beach, they pulled their bags. Pocket cafés, still a remaining photo processing shop that used be ubiquitous, a dozen modest guesthouses and rooms, two small art galleries, a Toko Oleh-Oleh full of souvenirs. Not quite to the beach, they enquired and accepted at the Puri Bali Hotel, which was a set of spaced-out bungalows.

Then, hungry, they walked back to the rumah makan, the little food joint with the bold claim outside. "We Have Aussie Ice Coffee".

'Punya sate lilit?'

'Ya. Punya.'

'Good. Two, please.'

The satay order went back to the kitchen, as always in Indonesia on a written slip. The lass came back with a basket of krupuk crackers, and Anne quizzed her on the iced coffee boast.

'Many Australie people come here. Some people ask us for ice coffee, and they sometimes did not like our ice coffee.'

'How did you make your coffee?'

'Nescafe,' she said. 'Nescafe is good coffee, no? With es and water.'

'Your customers did not like that? In some countries, that is how iced coffee is made, just coffee with ice.'

                    BALI in its MIDDLE AGES

'One woman give me a new resep,' she said, beaming. 'Aussie resep.'

He grinned. 'OK, tell us your good Aussie resep.'

'We buy small espresso machine. So we use coffee, small.' A finger and thumb measured an inch. 'So then we fill with milk, cold, and es krim and krim. So we buy cream, in a can. Pffff.' She looked pleased, and mimed a can press with her finger. 'So, we put ice in and stir it up.'

'That sounds excellent,' said Anne.'

'No, no. So we add more ice cream and cream on top and not stir. So that our Aussie resep. And a long spoon.'

She went back to the kitchen.

He looked at Anne. 'She's nailed it.'

'Bagus sekali,' said Anne when the waiter returned with the food. 'Resep betul. It's correct, Good Aussie recipe. We want two please.'

Again, she raced off.

'They are so desperate.'

'Can you see those two jugs on her counter?'

He walked over to the counter to check. 'Jamu Bali. By the glass. One ginger and one turmeric.'

She already knew.

'There's internet, too, See over there?'

In the morning, he headed towards the beach.

'You on a mission?'

There in their same street not three hundred metres away was the temple with its wall sculptures.

'Hmmm, I see what you meant.'

'Have you ever seen the Ramayana play?' It would have to have been before they met.

'In Denpasar with Mrs Faulding,' she said. Four decades ago.

'For hours and hours?'

'I don't remember that. No, I dare say a shorter version.'

'Well, I don't know if this is Ramayana or another Hindu story, but it reminds me. Monster people, people trying to avoid being tortured, fearful scenes.'

A boar with great tusks in the first panel was tearing off the clothes of a crying maiden, and a centipede creature half a metre long was chewing the breast of another. What the lactating mother pig was eating out on the next damsel might have been the scene he had pulled Rebecca from back then.

                              BALI in its MIDDLE AGES

The huge-toothed and big-bellied monster was throttling a young child, and another was stomping on two babies. Saws and curved ceremonial knives were chopping off whole limbs. Torture by fire was played out in various formats, and a hammer was smashing skulls. In the final panel, a tiger was devouring a body.

'Oh dear,' she said. 'The ogres are male. The victims are women and children. Always.'

He wasn't sure on that. Maybe they had it wrong. Was it the Barong dance's wicked Rangda, the Balinese queen of the witches, who was causing that evil and havoc? How does a bule, with no grounding in this old culture, interpret such storylines? In his day, Hell was simple—it was one overall fire.

———

Munduk was a small ridgetop village high in the hills south of Lovina. It had been a Dutch highlands retreat for the colonial administrators of Singaraja.

They checked into the Guru Ratna Homestay, the oldest building from those imperial days. It sat high on a dramatic ridge with wide views to the south.

A Bali-food cooking class by day, a guided introduction to eating a durian at sunset, then a long day walk to several waterfalls in the hillside and a satay meal with the family. This was easy Bali, a travellers' Bali. And durian was conquered.

What was not so easy was finding a drive back south for an airport escape. The only other gathering spot was one warung down the hill, closed most of the time. Passing cars were few, potential drivers were not in sight. His old way of walking out and finding a driver was becoming harder.

Bridge to Ridge

They had not learned the lesson. Last time they flew to Bali via Kuala Lumpur. This time they flew Scoot and came through Singapore. They again drove two airports away to catch the flight, rather than to Brisbane one city away, or local Maroochydore domestic if they took a flight change at Sydney. Also, it cost a night away before the first flight, and a night in Singapore.

It was the same excuse as before, saving a few dollars, but it was still a nutty idea.

Yesterday they had taken a taxi straight from the Denpasar Airport to a booked night in a Sanur guesthouse, to be poised for the boat in the morning. That was a third overnight of "not being there yet".

At least they had time yesterday to obtain tickets for the short ride today to Lembongan Island. Even that move wasn't smart—some tickets sold today at the jetty were cheaper. If only they had had more trust.

On Nusa Lembongan, the ferry-boat offered a free car shuttle. The car driver shrugged. Another traveller not knowing where they were. North or south? Coin-toss time. North. But then they got out after a kilometre. From that main road parallel to the beach they rumbled their bags on the cobbles of the first access track to the water, to Jungut Batu Beach. At the seafront, they walked past two accommodations, liked the look of the third, walked in, looked, asked, accepted, paid three nights.

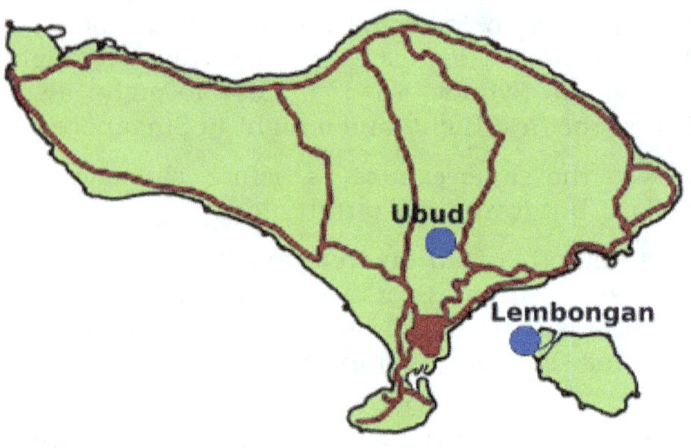

Their Made Inn room looked down six metres over the sandy foottrack onto the sea.

'Notice something?' he said, looking across the water.

'I notice it's quiet. I notice I like this place. I notice Mount Agung on the mainland sits way out at the right with cloud on its point.'

'No one has touted for our custom,' was his answer.

He looked out to Agung. 'That little hill frightened us one year, was blowing its top.' They had cancelled that trip and rebooked their Jetstar then to Phu Quok Island in Vietnam.

Anne stirred early.

'It's noisy out there.'

He rose and looked below.

'Two outrigger boats have beached below us. Bigger than the fishing outriggers. And lots of people are moving around and chattering.'

'Wish they'd be quieter,' she said. 'I'm feeling crook. Trying to sleep, but I can't.'

Stepping onto the deck, he closed the glass door.

The boats were transports, loaded with boxes and wrapped parcels, many baskets of vegetable, a box with protesting chickens, bottles of drink, and the ubiquitous plastic bottles of fuel. The scene at the water's edge was an instant market. The locals—all women—were buying, loading their goods into their baskets to carry home on their heads.

By an hour, the buyer crowd was dispersing. Getting hungry, he went inside to check on Anne.

Anne lost two days of Jungut Batu to the "Bali Belly". Over-cautious, she resorted to using the antibiotics they carried, taking no chances so far from home.

'It's not fair,' she said.

'Yeah, but we both know that fair has no meaning. Things can happen for no good reason. Travel to alien places, and alien mishaps turn up sometimes.'

She nodded. 'My girlfriend's solution is never travel, take no risks.'

She smiled a wan and wistful smile. He understood that.

And last year at Candidasa it was he who, on his birthday dinner out, had turned green and had gone to bed for two days. He wasn't about to remind her.

He added an extra day here.

———

Adi Bungalows at Mushroom Beach down south of the jetty was not facing the beach, but on yesterday's walk to here and then back to Jungut Batu they fell for the look of the grass-roofed, high-set huts.

All the vehicles on Lembongan were small trucks or motorbikes. Beyond the ferryboat shuttle car, regular cars were absent here, so three motorbikes pillioned them and their bags from their beach view to Mushroom Beach.

Aircon, at least until midnight, hah. Pool, yes. Coffee, bar and food in-house. Two hundred metres to an interesting snorkel-boat harbour and a dramatic lookout restaurant on the cliff where they'd lunched yesterday, ahh.

But there was one fail. Huts with grass-

thatched high A-frame roof-cum-walls look so cute. But as insulation, they were porous. No wind came in, but the heat leaked straight through. The air-conditioner, that saviour of weakling foreign tourists, was no match for the insistent heat of a Bali day.

Which, curiously, provokes another topic. So Lembongan is an island of Bali, not far off the Bali mainland? That is not how the locals read it. To the Lembongan people, Lembongan is NOT Bali. Bali is their neighbour, that's all.

On special overnight order, breakfast was sticky black rice porridge.

To hire a motorbike was $5 a day. No questions or checks here. Not one police person on Lembongan. Adi Bungalows had two bikes waiting each day.

'I tried this game once, long back.'

'Let's try it again.'

But this machine wasn't what he knew. It was a "scooter". This had automatic gearing and electric start!

Carefully and with a few unplanned wobbles he took his pillion on a circuit of Lembongan. In ninety minutes, seeing little traffic, they had been up to the north and down the other side, past some remaining plots of old seaweed farming, and had arrived at the "Yellow Bridge". In a tiny way,

   BALI in its MIDDLE AGES

this bridge was famous. He'd seen photos. It was known to those who needed to know, the biker-surfers who island-hopped onto Nusa Ceningan. The Yellow Bridge was one scooter wide.

She got off. She walked across. He drove slowly over. They rode on to the north of Ceningan. That was enough.

'Rattled?'

He nodded. Same question as Christy.

By early afternoon the scooter was back at Adi in Mushroom Beach.

'Besok juga?'

'Again tomorrow? Tidak, terima kasih.'

'Feeling older?' she asked.

At one of the tables, they sat and signalled for an order.

'Yes. But, more so, out of practice. I've not ridden a bike for more than thirty years.'

'We lived.'

'This living will kill us one day.'

'I'll shout you to sunset dinner on the cliff tonight, and you can take me on the snorkel tour boat tomorrow.'

Correction. This living is OK.

Their **nasi goreng** arrived.

'Not bad. And still at $2 a meal for this,' he said. For years they had used that meal as a pricing benchmark across Bali.

'The snorkel boat? Better book it today. Around Lembongan to north of that bridge?'

They strolled down to the beach and registered the boat trip. A noisy gathering of men was in a corner of the street, which was also the edge of the beach, to their south. Several rooster cages were positioned nearby.

'Hello, hello. We have an event.'

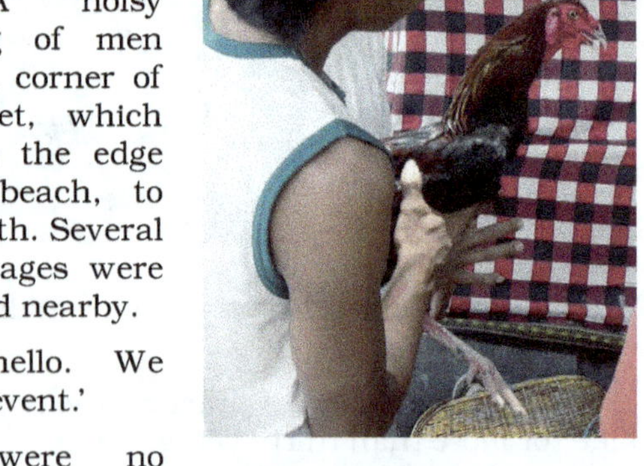

There were no other tourists about, and Anne was the only female at all. The men tolerated their presence, or rather, their presence was carefully not acknowledged.

Two birds were being prepared, their feathers smoothed, blades being strapped behind their feet, like a deadly reverse extra spur.

The cocks, colourful, groomed—and now armed— were brought to face each other, to set their aggressions started, and they were then thrown together onto the big woven mat that defined their arena. In an intermittent flurry of feathers, attacks and withdrawals, feints and clawings, and then sprays of red, the battle went on. The urgings from the men carried the length of the beach. One bird showed more damage, bled more, and the two owners pulled their birds from the contest.

Rolls of money changed hands, a lot of money. Or at least a lot of noisy transactions. But Indonesian rupiah can have a different value from the same count of dollar notes.

'I know there is a reputation of cockfights in Bali, and the cages of their darlings are everywhere, but I've not seen a fight before,' he said as they walked home.

'I hadn't even heard of anyone else who claims to have ever seen one,' she said.

———

Back into Ubud, as always, they targeted where they were last time, Monkey Forest Road as their starting point. The Ibunda Bungalows was easy, just alongside the Warsa of last visit.

Again, as always, they sat nearby with a coffee overlooking the rice-fields, awaiting this time two nasi plecing. In Hindu Bali, pork is sometimes eaten. It is beef that can be more difficult to find.

'I've been on the lookout for a gado-gado,' he said. 'Haven't had one for ages.'

'You won't find it often here.'

'Why is that? It's gone out of fashion?'

'No. Gada-gado is a Javanese food. Not so often in Bali.'

For a few moments, he was quiet. That warung in Manly Vale? The Bali Spoon. Twenty-five years ago.

'It's been a con.'

'Whatever works,' she said. 'You ready for the top walk tomorrow?'

'As always,' he said.

'But Monkey Forest is getting stale,' she said. 'We should be more adventurous next time.'

Wasn't Cahaya Dewata with Becc trying to be adventurous? Was that place still there now?

Hatted, shod in walkers, sun-cream in pocket, they stopped a few doors north, past Ubud's **Toko Jamu** and in front of one of the many restaurants, the ones all opening at rear to the remaining rice-fields. An animal lounged upon the counter at the street. It wore a collar and lead of leather. By day, it "lived" on that counter.

A big lazy cat? An otter away from home? A possum? Fox? Its fur was grey, with attractive markings, and its long-whiskered snout was more pointed than any cat's.

The Balinese waiter came forward with a cheshire grin. 'It is a civet,' he said in impeccable wording, and pronouncing civet as the English would. 'We make our special coffee by roasting the fermented beans from the civet. It won't hurt you.'

The animal moved its head nearer to Anne. She looked at the waiter. Tentatively, she reached to pat the head of the civet, which stretched in appreciation. It rolled sideways and looked her in the eye.

'You gave our luwak beans to Rebecca last year. Has she tried them?'

'I didn't tell you? Last time I flew down, I asked the same question. She hadn't dared, so we agreed to try it right then. She got it from her freezer, ground it and brewed it and we had a cup each.'

'And?'

'One cup in a lifetime was good. Two would be too much.'

'How come I wasn't told?'

They continued up the hill, went down to beside the Campuhan bridge, and began the climb up the ridge track, past the Downward Dog yoga rooms, a tiny new bush guesthouse, a café that wasn't open, and they headed for that warung that they recalled served the good coffee, up high and looking down. They might stay an hour or two.

'Our pilgrimage,' he said.

     BALI in its MIDDLE AGES

At School

Landing into Denpasar Airport, he took a taxi to Ubud, to the inexpensive Candra Asri Bungalows on Hanoman Road.

Driving right through Denpasar city and up the slopes towards Ubud was on every visit a shock. It was a remembering of how the traffic was slow and noisy, the roads were bumpy, and so many of the shops and shacks were so "Asian", poor, unpainted, small and generally dirty.

How could so many people live in such limited space? If one had forgotten it all since last visit, then here it was again, the great tumble and hustle of a people struggling to make life work.

Candra Asri turned out to be a good choice for a two-day stop. The bungalows and rooms were to the back and facing those same remaining rice-fields, as were all the hotels along here, and a comfortable café was on the corner opposite on the laneway.

He could do some preparatory study, find food and a drink, go for predictable street walks, and otherwise sit still. Ubud he had been to so many times before.

Late on his full day in Ubud, he walked out of town west on the main road, Jalan Raya, and this time down across the Campuhan River bridge. He started his long haul uphill. The road followed that next ridge up. Could he recognise the resort where he and Rebecca had stayed thirty years earlier? His memory stumbled. In those days, alone in the place, they had looked across westwards to the most beautiful of steep rice paddies in the Ayung River valley, next of the river canyons. They had walked that lonely foottrack up to a spectacular petite café each day for a cool drink and yet more view. He became lost in the reverie.

But now nothing was familiar. It was all Bali, but it was more populated now with hotels, cafés, resorts and a large shopping centre. No names rang any bells, and it was obvious that Bali progress can in short order wash away places that had once been precious. It was all so long ago. Had he misjudged how far from Ubud town they had stayed? And he hadn't walked far enough today?

He walked back down the road, crossed the bridge, and settled back to a Bintang at his café alongside the Candra Asri.

Then he stood outside at the roadside and watched and waited. Waited to spot any loitering person connected to a parked car. He approached one and got no result, but the second driver was willing to quote a car transfer to Padangbai on the morrow. A deal was agreed for 9 am. It was working again.

At Padangbai the driver left him at the Topi Inn.

Once again, Jack had no clear agenda in being there. It was another opportunistic pause, some spare days before next Monday, when he should be in Mataram.

Topi Inn was a funny place, established some time ago by a Dutchman, and it carried a continental informal style that a straight Balinese place would never get the same. Like many places here it was both a garden café and an accommodation, but this was no losmen, not bungalow. All felt wooden and garden, with little of the volcanic brick and rendered fencing. It did have some stone work, some fencing, but it didn't feel like it. Something felt not the regular Bali premises. How do you put figures and proofs onto "vibe"?

Viewed from the café, the rear upstairs deck seemed like a mezzanine space, and not a set of formal rooms. Go upstairs, and it was divided, with a large open space, then a family room, and a couple of smaller rooms at the back. Guests could be sleeping in any of those spaces, even with no more than a mat on the open deck, at the appropriate night tariff.

One of the small rooms was his, with light, thin walls and no aircon. No aircon? But then this was right on the coast. The bed was the sitting space for the tiny desk. For two nights, it was all enough space to crash. The café with its European slices and good coffee made up for the hippie/nomad accommodation.

However, in that tiny room, he learned more of the Dutch language than he planned. At about 3 am, the phone rang, facebook Messenger ringtone. It was not his phone; it was in the room next door, same volume though.

'Hullo.'

He'd had jobs where colleagues lived on other continents. There had been family who lived around the world. Any etiquette he knew said to phone them in their daytime, their waking hours.

This call lasted forty minutes, unabashed, at full phone-talking volume, for all who shared the Topi mezzanine that night.

He rose for an earlier breakfast than his usual and sat downstairs, grumbling to himself over his pancake.

Until the vibe seeped back.

———

　　　BALI in its MIDDLE AGES

On the Saturday he caught a Gili Islands fast-boat that was scheduled its first stop at Senggigi, a holiday village on the western tip of Lombok. From Senggigi he would find a driver to get past Ampenan to the capital, Mataram, not a long trip.

Most passengers were headed to one of the Gili Island resort areas north of Lombok, because those places had the renowned diving reefs and dive schools. Only a few travellers had business in Lombok.

The Eka Jaya boat was powered by eight outboard motors. As with Bali's bus transport, luggage was lashed to the rooftop.

The fast-boat crosses to Lombok in about ninety minutes, not the five hours of the ferry, so young Western holiday-makers, in their hurry to the Gilis, and with too much money, always go by fast-boat. The ride can be bouncy, but it's a short one.

Some of these boats, all aluminium and modern, had been made in Hobart, Australia. Years ago he had some business with one of the Hobart boat-builders, so he had at least a minor interest.

Before they cast off, the inevitable loud music began. Do the Indonesian passengers like loud pop music, or do the transport providers imagine their Western tourists want it?

All eight outboards work together. They are racked to run and to steer together. But, half across, all eight motors stopped, and the boat began to wallow in the choppy and windy ocean. The music was stopped. This boat was stranded on the high seas on that mid-afternoon.

The crew of two tinkered and adjusted for an hour. He was uneasy. All passengers were becoming stressed.

Then one engine started up at half speed, and the boat chugged a slow trip directly to the nearest land on Lombok, some distance north of Senggigi.

All passengers were ordered ashore, wading through a couple of feet of sea. The crew unstrapped all the luggage and carried it piece by piece, wading waist-deep with it held high, to leave it on the sand for claiming.

                    BALI in its MIDDLE AGES

The message of the stranding spread, and after half an hour local people with vehicles began arriving offering transport. Some like him needed to go south. The Lombok-bound (ex-)passengers had the less-worse deal, a simpler task to solve. But most were the holiday crowd now needing to head north to the village of Bangsal, where they could find a short local Lombok-Gili ferry-boat.

Did this event have precedent? Maybe the boat company and the locals could cook up a rescue operation very fast. But no passengers were charged any fare for the rescue.

———

Why be headed to Mataram?

As a part-time diversion for the last few years, he had been studying at Sunshine Coast University. No hurry. Doing it for the enjoyment, or enjoying it at least after the shock had eased of re-entering a campus community after so long away. Into his mix, he began some units of Indonesian language, Bahasa Indonesia.

Then arose the opportunity to do some of that study as summer school in Lombok. The University of Mataram, often coded as "UNRAM", carried a respected language centre, and that included teaching Bahasa to foreigners.

A consortium of lesser-tier Australian Universities had established an agreement for their students to do accredited study at the Mataram language centre, and that scheme was tagged "RUILI". Indonesia does go overboard with acronyms, but RUILI is easy to guess: In English, Regional Universities Indonesian ...

In two days, a week past New Year, wet season, his six-week school was due to start.

————

He arrived to Mataram in a car he had organised at the first warung on the road into Senggigi. Two of the rescued passengers had shared their versions of their story over a kopi Lombok, and then the owner was happy to drive them on.

His six weeks at Werdhi Guesthouse he had already booked. The price was OK and the photos online at booking.com had looked fine. It would be a moderate walk to school each day, but that meant worthwhile exercise.

Werdhi had five rooms. He could choose his room, and suspecting nothing he made his choice. By first dawn, he found he was nearest to the rooster in the neighbour's yard. From his upper level and over the cement-brick fence he could see the birds, the chickens and their crowing cock.

The ibu was Ayu, a successful Balinese entrepreneur, running a fine hostel business, comfortable, well-functioning.

Lombok, to the first approximation, is a Muslim-majority community. However, there is also a sizeable minority of Balinese Hindu people, and the Werdhi is plumb in the middle of a strong Hindu area, complete with a major temple one street away. Werdhi was Hindu environment, but the qibla arrow on the ceiling corner still pointed to Mecca.

Ibu Ayu's partner was businessman Nyoman, who spent considerable time in Jakarta, leaving Ayu the hostel control.

By Monday, the start of college, four of Werdhi's rooms had Australian students for the summer school. Ayu offered them a ride to school in her people-mover vehicle. The Werdhi contingent had hit the jackpot. The free rides with her or her driver became a permanent perk.

———

Life at school, at the Pusat Bahasa language school, followed routines quite unlike the aloof Australian version of academic classes.

The classrooms—two year-levels of class were running at the same time—had none of the regular installed seat-and-desk furniture he had grown accustomed to. The chair and desk were one compact combination unit, the table part being a one-sided wraparound. This was a grade schooler's desk.

There was no high-tech, more whiteboard and plenty of stick-up poster sheets.

An outright lecture, with teacher pontificating and dutiful students being quiet, was rare. Most sessions were more of guided and interactive tutorial.

So this was how Indonesians taught and learned. Part of that promise of "immersive".

Were the students examined? Yes. And their marks found their way to the faculties in Australia. Was the language structure delivered, the grammar subtleties? Yes. Did the teachers have passion and humour? No question. Could the activities be called varied? A lot more than at home. All the teachers turned up on Australia Day in late January with Aussie flags tattooed to their faces.

One afternoon each week a special outside adventure or class trip or assignment was arranged. A market visit to practice bargaining, a trip to the Baloq Sade  orphanage to talk with the children, the weaving factory, an evening out for an Arabian Nights

     BALI in its MIDDLE AGES

feast at AlHamra, an evening in with all preparing an Indonesian feast.

And hovering during classes and more so in the breaks, in the activity sessions, and after the day finished at lunchtime, were always half a dozen of the "Buddies of RUILI", the "Friends", local English language graduates with time to give and friendship to share.

He was at junior school for adults, even for a few (very) senior. The simplest summary is this: it all worked a treat.

'The most outrageous,' he messaged home later, 'was me delivering a long tutorial, in Bahasa, on making a lemon meringue pie, what it looked like, tasted like, the ingredients and how much of each, making and rolling and cooking the crust, filling with the lemon custard, beating up the stiff meringue topping and finding a way to grill the top, everything. But there was a roomful of hungry people by the end.'

'You're a fake. Have you made one, ever?'

'No, but I've watched you. Have you ever made my spanakopita?'

———

The first week of school wasn't over before the call went out: meet after class at the new Rock Gili Café, a walk distance from the language centre.

Only one espresso coffee place existed in Mataram, in all Lombok, he had thought, in a laneway at the east side of Mataram's one and only Mall. An amused Ayu had given him directions to there a few days ago. By any local standards it was expensive. Not many local people went, except a few quite well dressed. It did have coffee, pleasant coffee, but the place "didn't work".

Rock Gili trounced the Mataram Mall café. Modern, good coffee, décor simple, non-ostentatious Western, with Euro- and Indo-style sweet treats and savoury. And ordinary comfortable seating.

　　　　BALI in its MIDDLE AGES

Rock Gili also had coffee prices not unlike home, but the eats were cheaper, and it felt like a genuine lounging place to the Australian students.

The Buddies were slow to cotton on. They didn't go to coffee after school. But the students had found their "Uni Cafeteria" for gathering two or three times a week. They could share facebook contacts, plan weekend exploits or trips or assignations, discuss the classes. Compare SIM plans and pulsa payments for their phones. Gossip. Argue the merits of their home campuses. Perhaps dare to practice a sentence or two of Bahasa Indonesia.

Facebook was king. Email and text messages were out. Oh! The Messenger part of facebook he did know. Messenger could save on foreign phone calls. For a computer man, he felt dumb. Old.

He called Anne after that first Rock Gili gathering.

'You're all slow,' she taunted. 'Remember how fast we found your Topi Inn in Padangbai? And Mia Coffee at Hoi An in Vietnam? And several opposite the prince's palace near the market in Ubud?'

'Yeah, yeah. But wait, Ubud doesn't count for chasing coffee. Ubud has cafés all over, Mataram lives in a different century.'

———

Some community decisions appear to arise from nowhere at all. For the fourth weekend of the six weeks, a majority of the language class students decided to all decamp to Gili Meno, the central of the three diving resort islands north of Lombok.

On the Friday afternoon, they had hired several cars, despite it was prayer day, to get them to Bangsal port for the 5 o'clock boat, or the next, or anything tonight. To the foreigner, Bangsal office proved to be a difficult place to get clear directions, buy correct tickets, and to wait around feeling secure.

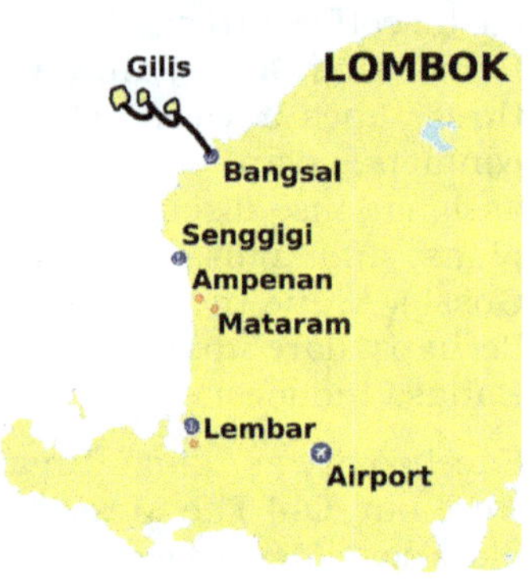

Until, finally ... 'Mas, mas, mas. That is your boat. Disana.' Half the language school mob didn't qualify as "Sir, sir, sir", but that was of less concern than knowing they had a departure happening, a wet-legs boarding on the beach sand, as there was no jetty.

The trip across the water was not long, calling first at Gili Air, and by thirty minutes all stood on the Gili Meno beach. Some started walking left or right. He checked his phone had signal. Their mob was dispersing. A couple had ambitions to join a dive boat tomorrow on the coral.

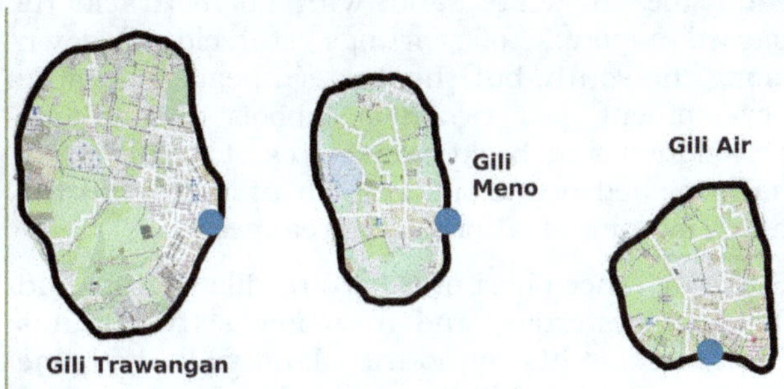

The Gilis have no cars and no scooters. He, Ricardo and Jess, all from Werdhi, negotiated with a cidomo driver—several had met the boat— to head a kilometre north towards the top of the island. Ricardo had a recommendation for good rooms.

'Too far. It feels away from everything. I'm walking back to the boat landing.' In the scale of this tiny island, a kilometre was far from the action.

No one had carried much, and walking back was easy. A bungalow room facing the beach was easy to negotiate. A hundred yards away was the large grass-thatched warung at the landing, the biggest venue on Meno. That made drinks and food for two days a lazy option, and made the likelihood of seeing familiar faces around a certainty.

Starting as the sun was rising, he walked alone clockwise around Meno. Most of the coastline had sandy beach, white sand, with no foottrack. He passed a couple of warungs, still closed, down along the south, but the western beach had little development, just two dive schools and a large abandoned and broken-down resort, with empty half-finished pools, one to each unit. Around the north, accommodation places reappeared.

Still a distance short of Ricardo's villa that he had declined yesterday, and now only sixty minutes from starting his round-the-island walk, he came to three cabanas built on the beach sand. Two bodies sat cross-legged on the middle one, facing the well-risen sun.

'Jack, hey.' It was Walter.

Walter had joined the language class for its second three-week half, and he also stayed at Werdhi Guesthouse. Mid-week he had been joined there by his girlfriend Ratna, and at Werdhi the others saw little of them.

But, for the next hour, the three sat on that cabana, and the sun rose higher and they could get some shade. Several outriggers came in from the sea to beach along to their right.

'You're not doing the Bahasa, I presume?'

She laughed. 'Jack, I'm from Jakarta. I'm here to be with my partner Walter.'

'But I thought he lived in Sydney.'

She sighed. 'And that is the biggest headache we live with at the moment.'

He waited.

'Walter works for an international NGO, but he's still based in Australia.'

'I'm in Indonesia sometimes, sometimes other countries,' said Walter. 'And Ratna is sometimes in Jakarta and sometimes in capitals of other countries in the world. We both love our jobs.'

'And we love each other. For four years now, since I had a posting for a year in Sydney.'

'You have a problem,' Jack said wryly.

'Yeah. We do a lot of travel. Or I do more of it,' said Walter. 'We get together wherever and whenever we can manage it, in whatever country works.'

'This week I have a few days leave,' she said. Her English was flawless. 'We make the most of it. For right now, the sunrise here works fine.'

A modern love story to write a book on.

————

Anne flew into Mataram on his final week. Ayu had fussed and the two had chatted a long while in Indonesian.

'This feels like Bali.'

'No. In this guesthouse, yes it feels like Bali. But Mataram city is more Muslim, gentle Muslim, more generic Indonesian. And it's a boring minor capital to a tourist expecting Bali.'

'But you have been describing all the fun.'

'We are a clan of Australian students taking over Mataram for a few weeks. We have an agenda, a reason to be here and to explore it. The locals are well aware we have invaded.'

'What, your wife has arrived here?' said Arum, the senior of the lecturers.

'Yesterday my guesthouse driver drove me to the airport to collect her. Today she's walking around and getting used to Mataram. But I told her it was still rambutan season at the markets, and she loves those. I presume she's prowling the streets trying to find some.'

                    BALI in its MIDDLE AGES

Then he spilled the story. Anne knew her Indonesian language better than he did yet. Or at least she could run a conversation in the street where he still struggled.

'Tomorrow, Anne is to come to our class,' Arum demanded.

'She is not signed up. She's not a current university student like the rest in the class.'

'**Tidak apa apa**,' she replied. Not any problem at all. 'We want her to come. Does she have a mobile phone I can call her on?'

'No local SIM. But we can text her.'

And for Tuesday through to Thursday, Anne slotted in ever-so-easily to the Level 1 language summer school in Lombok. Friday she would take off to recover, but joining the break-up party.

Wednesday was dress-up day, but they didn't know until they arrived and were met with a stack of sarongs. Well, it had been advertised as "immersive".

Anne disappeared with her choice, and re-entered minutes later with the sarong worn in Australian beach or bath mode, tied above the breasts. After one pirouette, she fled again and returned with all clothes back on, and the sarong about her waist as well.

Their teachers hadn't seen any of that, but the Aussies got the joke. Folk in the Muslim communities don't show bare shoulders. Even the Balinese commonly now don't. It's the same as no one wearing shorts here in Mataram either, he thought. The Australian men in the class had learned weeks ago to choose the lightest long trousers they had brought. This wasn't Bali.

Anne? She was now embarrassed.

———

Josef was a doctor from Tasmania, and not one of the younger language students. They walked with him into the Rock Gili. 'Let's sit over there, and you can tell us more.'

Joe ran Hobart's Poisons Clinic.

'I've been over here a handful of times,' he said, 'usually to Surabaya or Denpasar. Indonesia has an ongoing think tank on alcohol poisoning, trying to stem the many deaths each year from, particularly, the locally made arak.'

'In a mostly Muslim country?' said Anne.

'That makes no difference. People are people.'

'A week ago on Meno, I asked around and scored a bottle of brem,' said Jack. 'The waiter's family made their own. $10, and with a couple of friends it lasted the weekend.'

'Yes, brem won't hurt you, it's a mild rice wine along these islands, easy to down. There's also tuak that's made a lot, fermented palm resin, but that's an acquired taste. The Balinese often offer it at temple. But the arak is distilled tuak, a spirit like whiskey or brandy. Properly made, it's fine.'

'Joe, aren't all of those homebrew, bootleg?' she said.

Their lattes arrived.

'Yep. All drinkable alcohol is ethanol, fermented out of the sugar. But sometimes arak gets a proportion of a different alcohol, methanol. That's poisonous. If it doesn't kill you, it can still make you very sick.'

'And you've become the visiting expert?'

'Yep again. We need a lot of community education, because they'll never stop its production. And the medics here need better procedures for treating those coming in with symptoms. The Indonesian Government has paid for my summer school here, so I joined through the Uni of Tasmania. In a few days, my wife flies into Denpasar for her first time, and I'm going to show her the Java and Bali I have been running off to.'

———

After classes wound up, they had allowed for two weeks before they would fly home. They checked into the large Mascot Hotel at Senggigi village's beach, thirty minutes away.

They were room-bound. Outside was a downpour that made a river down every street. Suffering a drenching in the tropics was not the tragedy of a drenching in a cold climate, but—

'Plenty of time to make a plan?'

'A few days here. It's so like lots of Bali places, but add the mosque calls and a few extra foods available.'

'Can we go to your Gili Meno? It sounded perfect.' And Ubud. I love Ubud. Always.'

'OK. Ferry-boats from Bangsal. Uhh. Then a fast-boat right back to Padangbai and find a car.'

'We know Padangbai. Those cars are easy. They wait in the jetty carpark as the fast-boats come in.'

'That can work. This trip is not over yet.'

'Meno. Find me the brem.'

Back to School

'**I** want to talk with you,' she said.

'Huh? Yeah?' He was trying to wake.

'Your next summer school in Lombok starts after New Year. About the start of their Wet.'

'Yep.'

'So, last year I came and joined you there for your final few days of class.'

'You made quite a splash. The Wet had arrived. Then you plugged straight into our classes. Smartie!'

She kissed him.

'Why don't we do something daring for a time before the school starts? Early December is quiet, and Christmas is busy only for the prime tourist places like Bali. And we should still be before the wet season. I can leave you for home before you start school.'

'OK. Any ideas?

'Java? Borneo? We could see the orang utan.'

'Wherever we choose, it ought to be easy to finish into Lombok.'

'Well, Java could fit.'

'Java we have both been to. Not together, though.'

'Sumatra? Flights back to Lombok wouldn't be complicated. The jungles of Kalimantan? What is something that's new and different?'

He was awake now. A new project to be planned. He knew how to do that. How to plan trips that went where they wanted, but left everything flexible. Trips that cost not much, but delivered adventure. Supplied big experience, but didn't break the two bodies who were getting older.

———

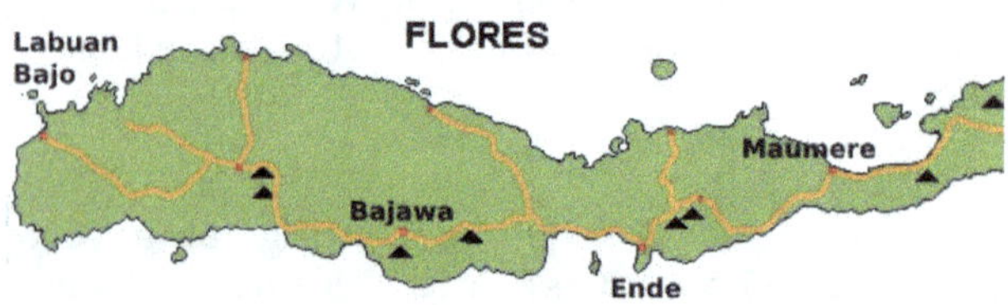

Via Bali, they flew into the large town of Maumere in Flores. Flores is the next large island eastwards along the Indonesian archipelago past Bali, Lombok, then Sumbawa. It would be a road trip back along Flores and a boat trip around Sumbawa and Lombok, to land at Senggigi in time for his classes.

     BALI in its MIDDLE AGES

For their three days in Maumere they had only two tasks, relax at a bungalow beside the sea, and find a driver with car.

Two tasks. But three things happened in Maumere. For days, they enjoyed lazing in the bungalow by the sea. Then a single driver called Filipe appeared as by magic, making bargaining a tad difficult. The third event was that Jack swiped at a large mosquito on his arm, making a big smear of tourist blood. The big adventure phase was due to begin.

While Java is Muslim, and some of Sumatra may be Muslim-er, and while Bali is Hindu and Lombok is Muslim with a mixture of Bali, Flores is different again. Flores had been a Portuguese colony, and it remains Katolik.

'But this Catholic-ness is so strong, such a contrast to the Indonesia I thought I knew,' said Anne. 'Filipe, apakah anda Katolik?'

'Yes, I am Katolik,' he replied.

'Everyone is Katolik?'

'Tidak. Flores is Katolik in the middle and it is Muslim near the coast. The fishermen sail between our islands, and many fishing families now are Muslim. But we are all friends.'

"All friends" usually works only approximately, thought Jack. However, Indonesia does hold its various religions together "approximately".

There was another thing about Flores that became apparent as they drove. Along the 450km length sat eleven "Type-A" (very active) volcanoes, and some lesser ones. Flores has one main road along the length, a rough and broken road often shaken or bombarded or fractured.

So they climbed to volcano craters, waited on roadblocks, and escaped by boat to tiny offshore islands to barbeque fish. They inspected the house in Ende where Independence leader Doctor Sukarno was exiled for years after the army coup and communist purge of '65. They visited Catholic churches and graveyards with colourful pictures of the Virgin and the Saints. And they stayed at recommendations always made by Filipe, because often not much else was available.

At Bajawa, they were led to Hotel Happy Happy, right on the main road and run by an old Dutch family who managed to stay after Independence.

                    BALI in its MIDDLE AGES

The plan was to stop for two nights. Was there any public museum or accessible exhibit on the Flores Hobbit, the early human remains that had been discovered nearby? The research was suggesting that homo floresiensis and modern homo sapiens might have lived together here for 30,000 years.

'Anne, I'm not very well,' he announced. That deteriorated, until he lay in a fever, sweating, hot, cold, near delirious, for several days. Filipe was discharged and paid out. Filipe had another driving contract to begin back at Maumere.

Medical treatment? Bajawa was a tiny place. He used their generic travellers' antibiotic, and they waited for the fever to break. Anne wandered the town and he stared at the qibla mark above him.

Five days late, they found a new driver and made a run for Labuan Bajo at the western end of the road. Four days remained before their contracted boat was to leave Labuan Bajo.

'This town is a model for Honoré, the fictional ex-French town in TV's **Death in Paradise,**' he said.

'No, this town has an Italian tone,' she replied. 'Italian food is everywhere.' And she was right. For reasons not clear, several Italian families had settled here over the years.

'It's still like that Honoré.'

'But Kuching in Borneo was also like Honoré?'

'Surrender,' he said.

'You're healthy enough,' she said.

———

Their boat carried twelve paying passengers. It had a practical common daytime cabin, but the sleeping deck, with sleeping bags for all, was just four feet high. The "heads" during the  night (through the dark) would be down the steel ladder. The first day, Christmas, they motored to Komodo Island and were escorted through the best viewing areas for observing the komodo dragons.

BALI in its MIDDLE AGES

'Goannas,' he said. 'But twice the size of our goannas.'

'Yeah. Impressive still.'

'OK.'

Onboard, the crew of two prepared an Indonesian galley meal, and all sat on the cabin floor on a rug spread for the purpose. Life might be good after all.

By nightfall, they were motoring across the north of Sumbawa. That's when the storm came in. The boat pitched and tossed without letting up for hours. In the dark, they both rummaged to find the "wafer" pills they carried, the military-grade (or so they were told) anti-sickness pills.

Let it be recorded, it was not a pretty night.

The sea had calmed by late morning. No one mentioned a breakfast.

'Announcement. Announcement.' In English.

'Everyone must change to another boat.'

They were on the high seas! Do they jump?

No, they pulled to a concrete jetty on a tiny island, were helped ashore—man-handled—from the front of the boat, and their bags were thrown to the jetty by the crew. No other boat was to be seen.

The crew now appeared to own no English. Anne didn't try with Indonesian. They waited, and in an hour a fresh boat appeared and took them aboard.

The new crew made the simplest of apology and announced they would put the travellers ashore this afternoon at Labuhan Lombok Port on the east side of Lombok. A ferry port at the end of nowhere.

Anne went to war. 'Our contract says we are to go to Senggigi on the other side.' Half English, half Indonesian. They couldn't hide behind language.

This crew had no such contract with the passengers, so a compromise was reached. The new boat reached Bangsal in the north, where taxis loitered for the Lombok-bound. For those (everyone else) who wanted to reach the Gilis or

    BALI in its MIDDLE AGES

Bali, Bangsal left them close enough to a ferry-boat to continue on their way.

They scampered down to Werdhi Guesthouse in Mataram—Bali in exile—where their room booked a month ago awaited.

The day after tomorrow, Anne would fly via Denpasar to home, and he would fly directly to Kuala Lumpur, to return with a renewed visa. Those air tickets they had had since long ago. Life could resume as planned. He had arrived in time for another language summer school, this time Level Two.

———

He returned from his overnight in KL's Little India. His reset visa could be renewed in another month (once only) at the imigrasi office a walking distance from the Werdhi Guesthouse.

Tomorrow afternoon would be the formal introduction ceremony for this year's summer school. The location would not be on the Mataram University campus, but in a school building closer to Cakranegara.

'I know about the new school place this year,' said hostess Ayu. 'The distance from Werdhi is the same, but I will drive you all in each morning, as for last year.'

Of last year's mini-gang, Ricardo was already in, but there was no Jess yet. Werdhi had three new rooms, and three other summer school students were staying. The language school had earlier published a list of recommended accommodation places around Mataram suitable for student stays. The Balinese Werdhi was not listed, but that didn't stop several of the students finding their way to Werdhi anyway.

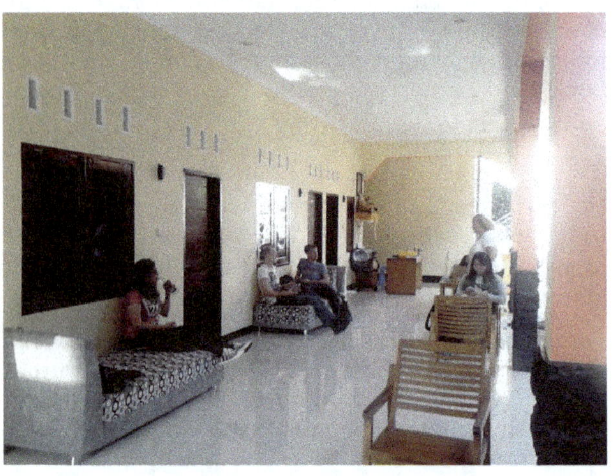

No matter. Those staying at other hotels or hostels learned over the weeks that the Werdhi contingent, captained by Ayu, led the best student life of them all.

                    BALI in its MIDDLE AGES

With the five long-stay students—at a good room rate—and a couple of rooms for more casual bookings, Werdhi was busy. Ayu did all her trading using the booking.com app on her Samsung tablet.

The Sunday afternoon ceremony had all the right personages speaking, all the best welcomes given, the practical instructions laid out for times, rooms and teachers. In that Indonesian way of no confrontation, no smell of dissension, what was not given was any reason for the shift of location and the missing proper sponsorship from Mataram University.

The host body here was no longer Universitas Mataram. It was a new entity. The teachers were the same people. The syllabus was to be the same. The same Friends of RUILI, the Buddies, the same faces as last year, all language graduates with time on their hands, hovered everywhere, as class tutor support and as social company afterwards.

Silently, over the twelve months, the universities in the RUILI scheme had recognised the old Mataram staff with the new popup Mataram Lingua Franca Institute (or "MaLFI") created to contain them. Any reference to the Mataram University was absent. There was no mention anywhere of what indigestion and hoop-jumping the Australian universities must have suffered in getting the academic approval in place quickly and so invisibly. New students knew no different, but those repeating from last year knew there had to be an untold story beneath. Conspiracy theories can be fun.

———

'You were lucky,' she said.

As early in the week as he could arrange, he had reported in to Dokter Adri, who was appointed as the summer school's medical support. Her clinic, a pretty cottage down a green lane, no Indo high fences, was not far from the school.

'Three weeks since the fever is now rather late for me to do blood tests,' she said. 'But I don't believe it was dengue fever.'

Two students in last year's cohort had caught dengue. They had spent a weekend on Gili Trawangan, the "party island", and they picked it up there.

'Here in the tropics, there are many more mosquito-borne fevers than dengue, and some don't have a name. From your story and your symptoms, it was one of those others. For now, remain alert for any recurrence. Get medical attention in that case.'

And if nothing returned, he was off scot-free.

The long Bali-style tiled terrace outside the three new Werdhi rooms served as a common room for the students, day after day. The three day-lounge sofas had communal use, and breakfasts often were a social event.

Late one afternoon in the first week, Ayu arrived with two durian fruit and laid out for a durian party. School finished about one, so by late afternoon most had drifted home. Likely, Ayu had waited for the "right" occasion.

'Durian? Oooh!'

'My mother grew them.'

'But you are from Bali?'

'I went home on Friday, mosque day, to see my family in Candidasa. The fast-boat from Senggigi makes it easy.'

'But are they not available at the local market here in the next street?'

'Yes, they are. But these were free.'

The odious durian smell was spreading, and they had not been cut open yet.

Ricardo appeared. Jack was older, by a lot, but Ricardo was taller and possessed that simple charisma that led to all looking to him.

'Durian?'

Again.

'Ayu has an offer for us all. A challenge,' said Renee.

Jack disappeared a moment and returned with two bottles of Hattens wine, Balinese. He'd beaten durian before today.

'Bali airport duty-free,' he said.

But that wasn't the truth. Two days ago, he had walked out along Mataram's main road to the Cakranegara end past the main markets. He'd been pointed to a tiny, discreet shop there, and they had asked for his foreign ID. The wine price finished the same as the Bali Airport price.

Ayu's son walked in, carrying a tray of lumpia, the Indonesian version of spring roll. 'If you pass the durian test,' she said. 'Durian smell and durian taste are not alike at all. When you are ready to try, you will be surprised. The taste is rich and pleasing.'

He knew all that.

'Enak?'

'Completely enak.'

'Let's do it,' said Ricardo.

She had her judgement correct. All five students and one of the casuals had now gathered around the table. They pulled up stools and a couple of beanbags, and began volubly to bargain their readiness to try this dangerous durian.

　　　　　　　　BALI in its MIDDLE AGES

The impromptu party lasted two hours. Only one held out against the dreaded smelly fruit, and the rest were surprised. More foods and drinks appeared with ease—it's out there in the carts on so many Indonesian streets—and no one went off to any separate dinner. There wasn't much study.

'Next Thursday,' she said, 'I want to take you, whoever is here, to the pearl showrooms. Lombok has some famous Black Tahitian pearls, and we can see how they are prepared into jewellery like necklaces and rings. You have no need to buy anything, but it will make a very interesting afternoon. Next week—'

He woke early and moved outside to lie on the sofa outside his door. The earliest direct rays of sun could be seen above on the trees. The hot water flask for tea had just been delivered.

The day-woman was already sweeping everywhere, cleaning away the leaves and rubbish —even yesterday's offerings if they still sat around, and if the dogs, cats and birds had left anything of those. Every home starts the day swept clean. She departed towards the kitchen.

Ayu glided in, as in a trance, and carrying a tray with a dozen of the Balinese offerings.

The first placement was one of the square woven coconut-palm-leaf boxes, holding flower petals of many colours, up onto the cast cement temple statue found in every Bali garden. She placed her offering to the gods on a ledge of the statue, added a burning incense stick, and drew her hand away, holding a petal, but with her fingers twirling like a Balinese dancer's. She reached down, took holy water in her fingers and sprinkled the offering.

She moved to the far step at the corner of the terrace, and placed another gift, rice set into a folded banana leaf. On the gate posts, she placed a frangipani flower and another of the square canang sari baskets. The demons must be banished, the ancestors should be honoured, and prosperity would be invited in. When she had finished her rounds, blessing every nook, she glided away, still in silence.

                    BALI in its MIDDLE AGES

So many, many times he had seen this same ceremony.

———

School settled into its familiar routine of morning classes and afternoons for study or leisure. Ayu each week arranged for "her" students to have an event or an outing. Visiting a sarong weaving centre. Attending a ceremony in Lombok's main Chinese Temple in Ampenan. Sitting by the Mataram Water Palace lake at dusk, all ordering bakso meatballs and spicy-chilli fruit rujak from the wheel-carts, the "five feet", the kaki lima.

At nights, he studied with his trusty Asus eee netbook, although the wifi was erratic and the data on the phone SIM was difficult in the evenings.

Jess, in her room—and sometimes she and Jack would sit studying in their silences together—had a different study style. The walls in her room were plastered with prompter pages, vocabulary and grammar hints. She had no PC.

Ricardo did have a laptop, but he spent most of his time with one of the Buddies, Wayan Balik, a Balinese young man. The two found good company, and Wayan Balik was more than happy to be talking Bahasa with Ricardo all the while, and sitting on Ricardo's terrace.

Jack concluded that Ricardo was the smartest student. His chosen style of self-made "immersion" with Wayan Balik served him well.

———

Sannia and Adi, two of the many Buddies, were close friends, always in each other's company.

Two cautions should be put on that observation. Firstly, Mataram is majority Muslim, and both of our couple appeared regular Muslim 20-somethings, full of fun yet being good convention-abiding people. Sannia, like several of the other women, wore her hijab scarf always. Secondly, how would this random, much older person of a foreign culture presume to assess the youth of Lombok?

'I can see those two becoming old Bapak and Ibu one day,' he said to Ricardo.

'I joked with them one day. On exactly that.'

'You're game.'

'They were both embarrassed. They denied the idea. They like being friends, they said. Simple.'

On Sunday, several of the students and some of the Friends all headed out to Ampenan Beach, the old colonial port. The students took a **cidomo** out —those carts Deanna had called **dokar**—for the adventure of it, and the Buddies scootered out, and all rendezvoused on the beachfront with its minor market. By an hour, the market's appeal was done for, watching the water was getting boring, swimming was not practical, and several people wandered off to return to their lodgings at or near Maratam proper.

Adi and Sannia, with Jack, offered to walk more in the Ampenan streets, looking for the old Dutch and Japanese and Independence-era buildings, the Chinese Temple, and other heritage sites that still stood. Ampenan had little role these years now that the current ferry port was south some distance at Lembar, the busy capital was at Mataram, and the beach had not much charm. The sea wall fell to deep water, not to any good sand for a beach.

Old Ampenan. How much could he recognise? He had forgotten that some of what was here was Japanese.

'Ampenan Port is where the Japanese fleet arrived from Java to Lombok and invaded us, and then captured the Dutch,' said Sannia.

Like their Sanur beach entry into Bali, he thought, not far straight across that water.

'Oil?'

'I think so. I learned they needed Indonesian oil. But Lombok doesn't have the oil. We had spices and sandalwood. We've been doing those for centuries.'

'Do you hate the Japanese?'

'I don't know. In three years, the Japanese freed us forever from the Dutch. My mother tells me all this. I was not here then, **Belum lahir!** Definitely, all that was before her time.

She stopped to look straight at him. 'Jack, you know our country's stories?'

'You are our neighbour.'

'We were taught Australians don't understand Indonesia.'

Adi had a call from home, and dashed off. Sannia and Jack walked a while more, and the day started closing.

Thus it became that he was riding pillion on the scooter behind Sannia, she in her hijab. Sannia, the good Muslim lass? —was unfazed. Jack the **bule**? —was struggling to hide his confusion. Were this Afghanistan, they would both have been shot by now.

'Hey, Pak,' she called back to him.

Hey, old fellow?

Pop?

It was high respect.

'We could stop at a good café before we get back. I know a good place.'

All the Buddies were learning by now that the Australian students placed a high value on their espresso, not the kopi Lombok or even Nescafe. They paid whatever it cost, and that was several times the local brew. The Buddies were getting the taste, too.

At the Rumah Makan Asri, they sat to eat and to drink their coffee. The offer being too good, Adi reappeared to join them.

The mosque call sounded out some distance away.

'That's part of your daily life? Do you go to the Friday prayers?'

Approximately, Mataram is closed down on Friday afternoons. Taxis can't be found, and many shops are tutup.

The second question she didn't answer.

'Yes, it's very much part of my life. I live next to our mosque.'

'Loud?'

'Ja.'

She stayed silent a moment.

'We don't talk about that. It is not correct ... not polite ... to discuss it.'

Was it a littler version of the national amnesia over the village-by-village country-wide massacres of 1965, that *Year of Living Dangerously?* Never talk about it, therefore it didn't happen. The million who vanished. When the Americans so wanted the communists and their sympathisers out, however done, and wouldn't mind a big share in the huge gold and oil assets either.

He remembered in time the maxim. "En route, you always pay for the driver's lunch."

———

Mataram Mall upstairs had a booth that made printed T-shirts to order. For ten minutes, he stood waiting there; he had a couple of designs— designs with attitude—that he wanted printed.

The afternoon attendant studiously declined to acknowledge the presence of this foreigner, wouldn't talk or even look or answer. Jack suffered this surreal scene for the while, and then wandered off.

'Selamat sore, Jack.'

It was Wayan Balik. They sat themselves in a mediocre café in the upstairs back corner of the mall. Two melancholy men.

Wayan Balik's family lived in a village on the northeast Bali coast. Now, he was in Mataram because "they don't understand me".

'It's Lynx,' he said. They had met a number of times, had bicycled up through the hills together, and he thought they were becoming strong friends, even maybe …

It hadn't been the only intrigue seen.

"Lynx"—they didn't believe it could be her genuine name—was one of the Aussie students. She had cut him off, wouldn't answer his calls, couldn't be found. Wayan Balik was miserable, not comprehending.

'Lynx is different,' Jack said. Lynx, a quite intelligent woman, was indeed different, different in class responses, different in reactions, opinionated, a person needing careful handling. Their Indonesian teachers, great teachers, didn't have any subtlety on non-conforming students, and he had seen their annoyance several times in class.

'I've learned to see it. Among my friends there have been some who live on a different part of life's spectrum. All good people, but eccentric or unpredictable.' Some translations to another culture can be difficult.

'How can I get her back?'

'Give her time. Be slow and patient. But very possibly you won't.'

He wished he could offer a better opinion.

———

'So you're going back home through Denpasar?' asked Suze. Most were exiting via Denpasar. 'But you are staying a few days?'

'Yes, I will,' he said. 'I want to walk the ridges above Ubud before I go home. Five days I have planned there in Ubud.'

Class was out for the afternoon. It was two days before their six weeks of summer school would be over. Ubud he always liked to include.

'I have a proposition for you,' she said. 'You shout me a coffee, a real one, and I'll explain.' She pressed her Fitbit to check the time. 'It's still early. Let's find our way back to the Rock Gili.'

The café was quite a walk across Mataram, to near UNRAM where last year's classes were held. There was heavy rain this morning, this was wet season, but now it was just hot.

'Hello, Nyoman, it's Jack. You're still running this place? Our school is further away this year, sorry.'

Nyoman was Balinese. A Balinese who had spent a year in Sydney learning his coffee.

Had she been having second thoughts? But two lattes later and two dadar gulung—those green rolled pancake desserts—and Suze was ready to explain.

'I've booked myself a Balinese driver to take me to Ubud on Saturday, paid him already. He'll drive me south again on Sunday for a Virgin flight to Sydney.'

Suzie was an adult woman, partner at home, and patently able to take initiative, get organised and stay safe.

'It's simple. I imagined it would be pleasant to have some company going up to Ubud. There's a lunch place in the rice-fields my driver has chosen for the trip up.'

Had she been planning how to ask with decorum and with no innuendo?

He looked at her and smiled. 'Look at you. I'm going to call you out. You look all unsure.'

She laughed. 'Yes, you're right. But Jack, I haven't been to Bali before. I transited two days in Singapore once, and otherwise I've been a Europe travel person.'

'You got yourself to Lombok.'

'Yes, I did. Sorry.'

'Sorry, nothing. Saturday morning's Lion Air?'

'Yes.'

'I accept your offer of company into Ubud. We'll enjoy it.'

He lifted his empty coffee cup in salute. She lifted hers.

Online, he had chosen himself a guesthouse one street east of Jalan Hanoman, not too far from the Hanoman–Monkey Forest Road corner. It had aircon, but not a pool. Oh well.

Suzie's place was on the busy Monkey Forest Road, not far uphill from the animal sanctuary, and hence not far from his guesthouse either. The driver had let them both out at her place. For him to then wheel his trolley bag two blocks would be no problem—he had done that for years of travel.

'There's a place called the "Yoga Barn" not far from here,' she said as they first organised her things along into her accommodation. 'I might look for it this afternoon. Do you want to share dinner tonight? Does your phone still have call credit?'

All the students had six weeks ago in Lombok fitted their phones with Indonesian SIMs. Any remaining pulsa credit was still usable in Bali. And they had the classful of facebook addresses still loaded.

'What's the time now?' She pressed her wrist. Gone two.

                    BALI in its MIDDLE AGES

'I reckon I'm going for my ridge walk this afternoon,' he said. '"Out in the mid-day sun," as the old colonial ditty said it, "Mad dogs" and all that. Should I make you a return proposition?'

'Perhaps you should. Better odds for good Bali fun than my idea.'

She readied herself for the trek. They walked his bag along past Le Petit Paris Café in the bottom bend of Monkey Forest Road, and half-promised themselves that dinner could be there. Lunch earlier had been comfortable company, the food great if expensive for his Bali, and the rice paddies, well-kept, had stretched out forever. Yes, dinner might be good.

They looked back again to assess the Paris. 'It might also be good for a cocktail,' he said. This was Bali, not Lombok, and alcohol was back on the menu.

He was low on rupiah, He should watch for an ATM as they walked.

He checked into his guesthouse, and got out his walking shoes and hat.

'Oh, look, these are the pearls I bought in Mataram. The Black Tahitians.' Two earrings in their gift box.

'She's a very lucky woman,' she said.

But the Campuhan Ridge beckoned.

For him, it was a familiar climb. Westwards on the main road, Jalan Raya, until short of the bridge. The Campuhan and several other rivers each ran southwards, leaving that geography of steep ridges and valleys all north-south. In the past, all that area held rice paddies, all contoured, engineered, to control the steady irrigation down to each farmer in turn. Nature had given Bali high mountains with seasonal great rains, and the Balinese over the centuries had tamed that gift of water with masterful and precise management. He was sounding like a tour guide. This walk, and especially in the wet season, was one of the true delights, for free, that the visitor could enjoy, that the locals could be proud of.

The lower parts of the trek had been tiled with concrete squares. The path felt more "official" than the faint foottrack of some years ago.

But every time he climbed up into this area, "progress" had taken more of its implacable toll. Less rice-field, more buildings—guesthouses, yoga clinics, cafés, even subdivisions with roads and houses further up. And more and larger buildings on the near horizon, westwards on the Campuhan Road on the next ridge.

The two cafés along the track had changed names. A new large one near the top of the walk was very well appointed. They sat there for an espresso and kue, something sweet. He hadn't arranged his rupiah, and that's all they took. Suze covered.

The lass who served them was an employee, he thought. Owners have a different presence, that innocent and comfortable pride. They hover a different way. This one was on day pay.

But the coffee was fine.

For a long time they sat, weary, meditative.

The wooden furniture was new and well-made. Bali does woodwork well, since colonial times or earlier, but this was modern, not old ethnic-feel Bali. The scene stretched down to the river hidden by its trees, and over the trees was the road north from Ubud, the noise of bikes and trucks carrying across.

Immediately below them were several huge rice-ponds, bounded as usual by their earthen walls. The ponds were full, but no rice was growing. Wrong season?

Thus far, he didn't know if it was all a tourist prop or genuine rice-farmer activity. It wasn't the narrow furrows of waterway; it was broader and flatter. What was not right?

'But Jack, look at all that construction along the left.'

He looked left. A four-foot-wide concrete path ran several hundred metres, the length of the ponds. A safety fence sat on one side, with timber posts and some cyclone wire. Halfway along was a tile-roofed Balinese rotunda or cabana and a high-quality Bali stone-worked altar/statue. Now, add a treated swimming pool and two padded lounge chairs.

'For a farmer?' she said.

The pathway continued to the end of the ponds, and there was built a complete new bungalow residence. The ultimate luxury of living in arrogance in the rice-fields.

Or is it no right of the foreigner to be making that judgement?

——— ——— ———

Ten months later, on one more island, Ratna picked them up on arrival at Havana Airport. Ratna who had stayed with Walter at Werdhi Guesthouse. Ratna on the cabana at the Gili Meno sunrise. Ratna of the Indonesian diplomatic corps.

She shepherded them through the Cuban customs and immigration areas, and the airport staff were familiar with her presence.

So slick was their escorted entrée that they neglected at the airport to change any cash into useful money, the Convertible Peso that is tied to the American dollar, and the only currency that foreigners were permitted to use. The streets were getting dark outside, and they arrived hungry, so it became a minor problem.

But from then, Jack and Anne's stay in La Habana enjoyed the company of a gracious friend, Cuba insights and guidance delivered in English or Spanish or Indonesian, variously, as they wished.

Was this the "international benefits" that the Lombok summer schools had promised?

'And Walter?'

'Walter was here two weeks ago, dos semanas,' she said. She closed her eyes and smiled. 'Dua minggu yang lalu.'

Sabbatical

It wasn't the book he wanted to be writing. It should be a grand vista of human confounding and alien confrontation, spanning the twenty-first century. His work would start with the troubling returns from NASA's Cassini Mission to the planets, throwing theological and military and existential disarray upon all humanity.

However, it deserved an introductory portion, he decided, harking back to the European Enlightenment, that earlier great disturber of ancient certainties.

So that's where the epic would start: Giovanni Cassini, seventeenth-century astronomer. The Galileo era.

There was a problem: the Giovanni Cassini prelude portion, when story-boarded out, was soon itself assuming the status of a full historical novel. OK. Write two.

Start with the first book. The old Italian. Telescopes. Cassini's "Vision". Good pun. The material was there. The real book could come later, the "Cassini Mission". The inter-planetary, inter-stellar military hunt for whoever was out there.

Plan: 1. Sit butt on chair. 2. Pick up pen. (Sorry, open up laptop.) 3. Write words. Write more.

After many months, he estimated he had a draft of ten percent of the planned novel. There would be no fortune and no fame at that rate. And it wasn't even the book he first planned to be writing.

Was life so full of disturbances and distractions? He lived by the sea and the river mouth. He could shop, watch a movie, go for top-grade walks all nearby. The sub-tropical climate of south Queensland was the envy of many. His employed life was long ago wound up.

Butt. Write.

———

At the airport, he put a SIM in his phone for $6 and reinstalled the Telkomsel app. His driver took him straight to Padangbai on Bali's southeast coast, the ferry and freighter harbour. The online booking was for the Serangan Inn II, half up the ridge sitting behind Padangbai.

Yes, the Inn had Roman numerals in its name. Not a Balinese thing. But in this language "Serangan Inn 2", with Arabic 2, could mean a plural, like Serangan Inn Serangan Inn, or Serangan several-Inns. Is there a Serangan I?

He had been here with Anne, and this was now his choice for a three-week writing sabbatical. To sit his butt.

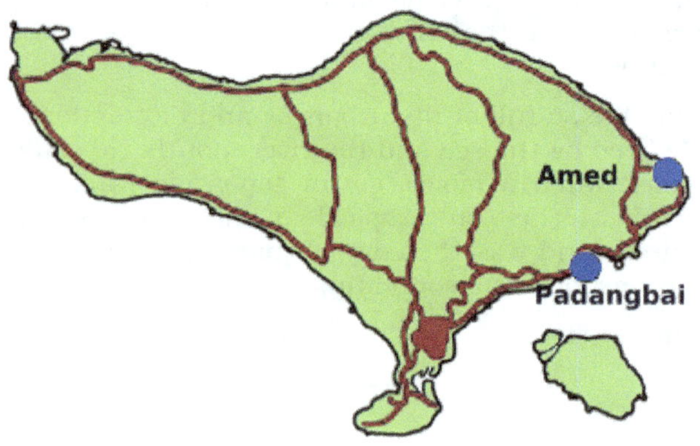

His room had that same panorama view he remembered—the town beach ahead, the whole port wharf on the right with its loading and departings through most of the available hours, and eastwards at left the headland holding the main temple. Then, below, warungs, satay stand, fast-boat jetty, a tiny nightclub, Topi Inn hidden down left, everything needed.

If he shut his door, all that vanished, and the keyboard remained.

                 BALI in its MIDDLE AGES

Leaning his elbow on the small desk, he rested his chin in his hand.

He was on a minor hillside in a lost ferry port on a small island. It was in a new nation of thousands more islands, a huge archipelago with once boundless wealth in spices, wealth that invited ruthless and avaricious colonial overlords for centuries.

The mobile rang.

'Good evening,' she said.

'Hi. You're up late.'

'Yes, I'm still preparing a class for tomorrow. I have seven people tomorrow. Tell me, how is it going? Have you put enough ink to paper?'

'Oh, remind me again. What is ink?'

But he rambled instead on ferry ports, Dutch spice traders, and the cobbling together post-war of many islands into one feisty people. His words tumbled across the oceans.

'Why do you chase such places?' She was laughing.

'Great history or big geography anywhere is always exciting.'

'Like?'

'Remember the floating grass islands in Lake Titicaca? Think of the slave quarters of the sugar plantations in Cuba's Trinidad.'

She stayed silent.

'Indian Garden down the bottom of the Grand Canyon. The medieval Medina of Fez, the cenote caves in Mexico, the old Cham-dynasty temples throughout Vietnam. Or the smuggler trails through the head-hunter jungles of Borneo.'

'Stop. Stop. You win.'

'The Galapagos giant tortoise.'

'Stop. Every last one of those was stunning.'

Jerusalem's Wall? No, she'd not been there.

'And, Jack,' she said, 'don't we go for the people? Their smiles and their stories and their generous friendship for a while?'

Desperately, he needed a sleep.

 BALI in its MIDDLE AGES

Mid-morning was often when the coffee urge arrived. Slinging the tablet and a keyboard in a carry bag, he headed for the Topi Inn. The venerable tiny eee netbook had been abandoned as now end-of-life, and he travelled with the large laptop that lived on his home desk—a risky idea. The tablet was the laptop's satellite.

1. Sit. As travellers find everywhere, wifi in cafés may be fine on one table and pitiful on another. Wifi was free, and free was cheaper than data from his phone SIM. Up high on Topi's wall, he could see the new modem, so he knew where to sit, because otherwise, in that lush garden, every location was a pleasure.

Rainy season hadn't arrived yet. It could be soon.

He was here yesterday. They recognised him. 'Pagi, Mister Jack. 'Morning, he said. If only he could remember names, even remember faces, like the Balinese could. Were the Dutch founders still involved with Topi? Water arrived. Oh, those old days, when all water was deadly dangerous. And the menu card. All still continental. The sun was getting higher, but the cloud cover broke all its stings. The shades and the leaves completed the protection, and a slow, moist breeze came from the beach, over the jumble of waiting fishing boats and diving tour boats, and across the dead-end road. Maritime noises called and rumbled from the ferry harbour across the water at the right.

The tablet battery would be good for a few hours.

Beside him in the Topi garden was a small pond, built of rock, running a motorised fountain, a single jet that kept up a rippling and tinkling of water.

3. Write. Words.

———

A Padangbai street map has six streets. The main drive coming into town goes directly to the wharf, and he had seen on occasion a kilometre queue of vehicles all throbbing and keen to roll aboard the next ferry.

Of the remaining five streets, the Serangan Inn II was on the next "main" arterial, Jalan Silayukti, allowing vehicles to skirt around the awkward fast-boat jetty carpark that cuts that street that ought run, maybe once ran, along all the town beach. Local traffic can thus access, past his Inn, the rest of the beach as far as the Topi and the temple. By Padangbai standards, he lived at a busy junction.

Early afternoon, a heavy truck drove past, the sort of vehicle never seen along here. It must have managed a turn in the usually busy carpark, because it returned and parked blocking the street for forty minutes. Five men at demon speed shovelled the truckload of dark volcanic sand out onto the street, and the truck left. Cars could again slip past, just, their wheels on one side riding onto the pile.

How many days would that stay? He looked down from the upper terrace outside his room and shook his head. He went back to his keyboard.

An hour later they started arriving. The junction was a three-way one, and they all came from up along the third way, a narrower lane. Men came, women came, youths came. Thirty, forty. A few kids, even. There was one barrow only, but they came with tarpaulins, with double-handled cane baskets, with plastic buckets, with dirty canvas packs that were worn on their backs. They scooped with spades, with lids, with pieces of wood. Before night fell, that roadside was cleared and swept clean.

He went downstairs and walked up the lane, and there was all that black sand inside the front of a guesthouse, ready for construction, for mortar, for rendering, for making bricks.

He should walk back to his laptop.

———

Padangbai faces dawn-ish. At first light, he rose and walked along the beachfront road past the fast-boat jetty that still slept and the Zen Hotel and the already-awake ferry terminal.

There were people walking, a couple of scooters heading to things important, and old Ibu Ketut setting up her fruit table past the jetty. Past the wharf entrance he strolled on, on to the south where there is an alternative Padangbai, with locals' houses, some quite smart, several laneways to mystery, and a few guesthouses that cost less because they don't belong near the town beach and are missing the postcard feeling.

He walked past the track he had been looking for. In his pocket, he did have a map, printed at home, but still he missed his turn. Backtracking, he discovered it, a foottrack behind a broken car barrier, and because the sign was so ambiguous he hadn't recognised what it said.

Up over a sandy rise he climbed, no further houses, just one tethered and startled cow. He needed a scramble in the early light down the sand to the beach itself. In all, it was a twenty-minute walk.

"Hidden Beach". Or that was one of its alias names. Quite well hidden.

Not a minute later, the sun's first edge broke above the sea. On the white sand, he sat a while. Tomorrow he must bring the camera.

A far ship inched leftwards on the horizon, and passed, hazy and shaking, under the sun as that fiery ball launched itself carefully clear of the water. The sun was bigger than the ship.

He had been wrong. ***Death in Paradise***'s Honoré town was Padangbai.

Today should be a productive day.

———

Two weeks in, saturated in the effort to be writing his great wisdom, he took a day off. A local driver offered a 500,000 rupiah ride—$50—to Amed, waiting around there for three or four hours, and returning to Padangbai.

Past Candidasa on the coast and old Amlapura city inland, they circled the coastal mountains to enter Amed from the northwest. Like the Lovina coastal beaches region, the Amed descriptor refers collectively to a stretch of ten or fifteen kilometres of beach villages. But unlike Lovina, there is an actual village named Amed at the north. All the villages have coastal peaks close inland, and beyond them, to Amed's west, is the towering and renegade volcano Mount Agung. No surprise that the beach sands are all volcanic black.

Friends at home had been encouraging them for years to visit Amed. In a month or two, after his writing experiment was all done, he and Anne must come again to "his" Padangbai and then Amed. Today was a scouting mission.

Parking in the carpark on the only street, south of Amed proper, and opposite the IndoMaret store, the driver planned to rest in the car, or walk on the beach, or find a shady tree, or whatever waiting drivers do. Jack would return to the car at 2:30.

Task 1. Is Amed area a good place to come with Anne? (Default answer. Anywhere was a good place to visit.)

Task 2. To Amed village itself, or to another of the villages? Jemeluk? Lipah? So far, these were just map entries.

Task 3. Choose one or more candidate accommodations for booking.

Answer 1. Already answered.

Answer 2. A dusty road on a hot Bali midday makes long-distance reconnoitring rather demanding, and café stops appealing. However, he walked some stretches of the black sand, where the beach frontage of many guesthouses and hotels showed terraces, pools and lounge chairs, and where several beach warungs sold coffee or local meals. Then, some places were seen better by approaching from the road. He wandered into a few places to look around or to ask their initial casual rate. Some said "resort" too loudly.

He got as far as the creek bridge at Jemeluk, and liked the look of the bungalows all crowded there and all busy.

But it was too hot, and he spent ninety minutes chatting, using some of his still-broken

Indonesian, with the coffee maker at The Cup Resto near where his driver would be waiting. Answers he didn't have; he had instead photos and some noted prices.

Answer 3. See Answer 2. His brain was fried.

So go back to Answer 1. Yes, they must come to Amed in February.

The driver reappeared on time, and they headed southwards down the coast road. Past Jemeluk some way, they passed several new resorts on the small cliffs on their right. Must look those up online, he thought. But anywhere would work.

———

The Jetstar flight to Brisbane was not going to leave on time. The mid-afternoon check-in queue, a long and annoyed one, had not been processing any tickets or baggage for three hours. Already it was the supposed boarding time. The only message down the lines was, "Not yet. Sorry. We have a problem."

The departure time on the boards was removed.

A while after the scheduled flight time, the desk started processing, but slowly. The staff were checking by hand the tickets and passports, recording the check-ins, taking the luggage. At least the luggage conveyors were still working.

He got beyond the security and X-ray and into the airport proper, the departure side. One board read depart in three hours. A second board had blank. It was 7 pm, and he sat in the food court for a croissant. For the flight, he hadn't pre-ordered food, and who knew when that flight would even be. The food court was full of Jetstar people; he recognised many faces. He messaged Anne in Queensland, though she must have left already to drive to Brisbane to collect him near midnight.

A woman came to share his small table, please. Sure.

'Veronica.'

'Hello … I'm Jack'

That was all. It was enough.

By an hour later, he had walked through to where Jetstar usually had its gates. The flight was listed, but nothing beyond "Delayed". No staff. He sat to read his tablet with the text of his nearly-there tome. Bored, then he ambled back to the busier central area, where there were bars and food, and wandered into the Duty Free store. A prominent notice read "Jetstar passengers can not buy duty free here." He wandered out and ran into Veronica.

'Hello again.'

Was she going to ignore him, or treat him as a suspicious stranger? Unless the male is one of those very charismatic types, this situation usually gives the call to the female.

'Oh, hello. It was Jack?'

'Yes. Have you found any good news?'

'Hmmm. No.'

At the Jetstar area and in the corridors near there, a couple of hundred people sat or stood bewildered still.

'Well, I did hear, not official, but they have a computer glitch all across Australia and reaching to here. And our plane hasn't left Adelaide yet.'

They sat in a bar and drank a couple of Bintang and a whiskey. He sent the airline update to Anne. After a few hours of safe story-telling in that bar, the two passengers walked up closer to the Jetstar gate to find some patches of carpet to sit on and wait out the night and catch some sleep.

The plane from Adelaide arrived into Denpasar nearing 9 am, by which time all the grumpy passengers had received and used their breakfast vouchers at the food court.

Among travellers, stories of airport hassles abound. He reckoned he'd always been the lucky passenger. "My luck was out this time," he texted. "but boarded now Cusoon."

—— —— ——

                    BALI in its MIDDLE AGES

The Postscript:

Cassini's Vision was published. Available everywhere.

It was a great read, with murder, famous paintings, sea pirates, licentious Venice courtesans, spies, witch burning, polyamory, an executed king, slavery, the speed of light, heresies and the Inquisition, life in space, the Pope's food recipes, medieval feminism, and a lot of false history, of late known as alternate facts. And some very threatening astronomy.

Astrology, too—is that different?

No garage is full of books: that is old technology. He does, though, have a couple of beautiful copies at home.

Otherwise, he believes his sister-in-law in Melbourne ordered a copy at her local bookshop, and it was duly delivered a week later, and she read it. On the grapevine, he heard she was scandalised.

Cassini's Mission is still a plan "for one day".

After two months, they returned.

The original era of the single backpack to service our two travellers had been long solved by having the 2-wheeled trolleys. They reckoned now that 7kg each of cabin baggage and one 20kg allowance across two trolley bags would be the most economical packing. What can fit in under 34kg? A lot, it seemed.

Bali is tropical, and heavy clothing needn't go in. If fancy nights out aren't planned, more clothing can be saved. If boots or gear for heavy sports aren't needed, again the pack can be lighter. If the washing is done as you go, the number of items needed is small.

What is the opposite of that? It's the tourist couple lugging around, with much huffing, a pair of 32kg maximum-spec checked-in suitcases. Ballgowns in there? Or three weeks of clothing to be all laundry by home time?

'So what does fit into 20kg checked?'

'Come and look at the pile.'

The neighbour, not much of a travelling person, cast an eye over the four bags on the bedroom floor, the items scattered around the room, items shoved onto the empty bags, all making walking anywhere very awkward.

The flight was tomorrow.

Take a look at a "his" version of the listing. A list of the chaos. No order yet, no grammar.

- ☑ Laptop, and its charger, cables, mouse, hub, and bluetooth mini-speaker (for sitting across the room watching ABC News online from home)
- ☑ (Bare) PC and anything with lithium batteries stickered with a reminder to go into cabin baggage
- ☑ The PC all configured with one browser holding his login passwords, another browser with her logins
- ☑ Registered with a VPN to be safe in hotel or café wifi environments
- ☑ With a VPN option to appear to be back in the home country to not alarm the bank or other apps
- ☑ His phone: a geek's phone, a tiny 4 inches long Unihertz Jelly, full Android but meant for tiny fingers
- ☑ Her phone: was her business office and her quality camera, and so much bigger, a Galaxy
- ☑ Two 5-volt power packs, several 5-volt chargers for phones and his tablet and her Fitbit, an assortment of usb cables, micro, mini, type-C
- ☑ Android tablet for reading and writing—earplugs for listening

☑ 12-ft 240-volt extension cable, wire as thin as legal, and two double adapters AU style, and 3 x 240-volt adapters Indo to AU

☑ Metal cup and 240-volt water boiler—for cheap places without a kettle

☑ One plastic plate and sheathed sharp knife (NOT to go in cabin bags)—for cutting fruit

☑ An old paperclip, to spring open the SIM tray on the phones—both phones will take a second SIM

☑ 2 plastic spoons, for just in case

☑ Scale to weigh all bags before flights

☑ Plastic ties for bag security—who needs US-approved "security" locks?

☑ Nail cutter to cut the ties on arrival—doesn't alarm the Xray screening like scissors—travels in outer pocket

☑ One mini padlock (2 keys) for any incidental bag lockup—nervous going out, want to lock up something?

☑ 2 or 3 rubber bands

☑ Snorkel goggles (each) and breathing tubes, but not the fins (too heavy, hire those)

☑ Small plastic water bottles (to be empty at security checkpoint)

☑ 10ft of cord and a dozen pegs—some laundry powder—flat circle of rubber as a multi-fit sink plug

☑ Small folding umbrella (not in cabin bags), two mini ponchos—for shit weather, even in Bali

☑ Pills for everyone, and prebiotics ("shelf-stable") and anti-gastro antibiotics and seasick "wafer" pills

☑ Hand sanitiser—5ml mini personal sprays and a refill quantity—not many travellers used these, but they had, for years

                    BALI in its MIDDLE AGES

☑ "His" shaver, charged—leave charger home
☑ Hearing aids and batteries—thinking small now—
   getting older sucks
☑ Exercise bands for keeping fit—for getting younger
   again
☑ Torch
☑ Pocketable zoom camera and spare batteries—and
   you imagined everyone now used only their phone!
☑ Spare shoulder bag that squeezes to size of a duck
   egg
☑ Toiletries case, a few mini-soaps just in case,
   shampoo, same, and all the rest
☑ Sunscreen 50 (that number keeps rising), insect
   pump-spray (abandoned every other method)—
   packed "under" and well-sealed in a ziplock bag
☑ Nail scissors—"under"—several weeks of growth can
   catch one out—but these also can open packets,
   trim advert junk from maps, cut string, chop soft
   drink bottles into whiskey glasses, open uht mini-
   milk, do many chores for a traveller
☑ Spare spectacles—because the main pair is old and
   ready to fail
☑ Anti-skim sleeves to protect credit/travel cards

What about clothes? "His"?

☑ Wear inflight the joggers, zip-apart trousers, long-
   sleeve shirt and cardigan—4 am at the airport, it can
   be rather cool
☑ 4 shirts/tops (1 with long sleeves)
☑ 2 more shorts
☑ 7 days knickers etc
☑ Swimmers

☑ Sarong, flat type, not sewn around, because those
  don't work well as a beach towel
☑ Mini (gym-size) towel
☑ Sandals for usual wear
☑ Some socks for the joggers for walking further
☑ Bag (branded "laundry") for pending laundry

Clothes "hers"? 'Hey, I'm a woman. We have a bit more.'

Stuff 20kg max between the 2 checked bags, 4kg max in each main cabin bag (which are tiny light frameless backpacks anyway). That leaves 2kg or 3kg for his shoulder bag and the lady's handbag, with the travel valuables, the following stuff that never leaves the person:

☑ Passport, eVOA visa documents and e-CustomsDec
☑ Streetside other wallet
☑ $1000 of convertible cash
☑ Travel cards from the bank
☑ Leftover old Indo banknotes
☑ Old maps from last time
☑ A phone each

Did you count the kilograms? 2 or 3 spare still? Funny, that spare always vanishes at the last minute, or at the airport. Hah, but duty-free weight doesn't count.

The final answer is this: In 34kg total, one outrageous heap of junk for two bodies can be smuggled abroad. Most trundles along behind, through an airport (easy) or along gravel or

                    BALI in its MIDDLE AGES

cobbled streets and garden tracks, sometimes a very long way.

The wheels on those trolleys? They get a brutal life. Over the years, two sets of trolley wheels had been replaced. First set: at a travel shop in Vietnam. Second: Ebay to the rescue, replaced at home. For a third bag in Mexico City (or was it Havana?) they found no wheel repair answer, and they bought a complete new bag.

Mr Author, the chaos has spread. Your writing has gone more downhill. The list should be properly written down, organised, printed neatly, ready for next time.

And you should be listening again to more of the "Grammar Girl" podcasts. "GG" has a Fogarty name, and that was your own mother's surname. So smarten up. Your editor will be getting frantic.

He looked at their pile of "stuff" that was to go to Bali. He had a big pride once in travelling minimalist. When, oh where, did that change to this?

He should shove it all in, unsorted.

———

Meanwhile, China was on the defensive. Captain Trump was lambasting the Chinese laboratories, their markets, their border controls, their theft of all good and honest things American.

Some countries had closed their borders, shut their airlines to certain passengers. The world was getting nervous, holding its breath. Bat virus? Pangolin bug? Another world typhoid fever?

Or was it all a vast overreaction, a boon for conspirators?

Indonesia was insisting they had no SARS virus in their country.

———

The car from Denpasar Airport brought them straight across the island to Padangbai. Direct to the Kembar Inn on the beachfront road and a hundred metres from the Topi Inn.

'Spend three days in my town,' he said.

'Yeah, OK. I've been here, up that hill, but I'll play the game.'

Next morning, they passed the fruit stall by the jetty. Old Missus Ketut.

'I know him,' the woman said to Anne, and she smiled. It was the first of several recognitions around the town.

     BALI in its MIDDLE AGES

'Saya juga berkenal dia,' Anne said, smiling back. 'I know him too: he is my husband. He has been writing his book here. Menulis buku.'

'He buys my fruit.' Ketut had been his daily source of tiny bananas, the pisang. And today he saw she had his favourite salak snakeskin fruit.

They've decided this old foreign bloke who was hanging around their town for weeks must be OK after all, he thought.

They spent the few days traipsing over the places he had enjoyed on his sabbatical. Was all that why the written words had been so slow coming?

They walked the "shorter way" over the headland with its temple, to the coral beach, the Blue Lagoon. The beach warung there was not open. He'd never seen it open. They didn't swim, and the return walk was detoured into the Topi Inn.

At dawn next day, they hurried to the Hidden Beach to catch his magic sunrise. On the same track, the same Bali standard cow grazed. Or its calf.

Then they were on the beach alone. 'I saw a photo shoot here one morning.'

'Professional photography?'

'Didn't look to be. She had flowing robes and blowing hair, and the rising sun made a great backdrop and interesting light. But they wouldn't say much when I tried to talk. An influencer or Instagrammer trying something out. And enjoying it.' They hadn't needed him.

'Maybe they were simply a romantic couple.'

He pointed along the beach. 'Come, I want to show you something.'

They walked onto the rocky ledges at the south end of the short beach. Not much above the sea level, and the sea waves were breaking adjacent.

A subterranean roar started, and the rock they stood on shook.

'Aaaah!' she cried. 'What's this?'

'An underwater cave. I discovered it.' He couldn't have been the first!

'An inrush of wave water that often makes blowholes blow. But there is no blowhole.'

                    BALI in its MIDDLE AGES

A place they both grieved for was Warung Sinar that nine years ago they had so enjoyed. The locals ate fabulous seafood there, and that spoke loud. Sinar had been at the beach end of Jalan Silayukti, the Serangan II street, but now a dive tour office sat there. Progress.

———

From Padangbai, he booked two nights at the Anda Amed Villa Resort, rather south of Amed and Jemeluk villages. It sat on a minor cliff face on the inland side of the road. But it did have the sea view and, as now becoming so common, an infinity pool. There was no claim to being beachfront. Wonderful place—new, elegant, comfortable. Reception staff could move to the bar and serve a cocktail or a Bintang or a coffee.

But no one else was staying there.

Dinner was at the Gusto restaurant next door, also positioned on the rise, and run by two Hungarians, and having some European treats not expected in Bali.

That was all quality. But there was nothing more nearby.

'Got it wrong,' he confessed. His "homework" of two months ago was awarded a "fail".

In the morning, they walked an hour into the Jemeluk-Amed beachfront area, sampled the coffees, bargained a satisfactory room price at Pakel Villas at the far end, Amed itself, and arranged a transfer car for the morrow.

Five nights at Pakel's was two stars lower, $12 cheaper, and three notches more to their liking. The upper-level sea view room, obligatory tiled balcony watching over the black sand beach, the tiny warung on the beach at the foot of their own steps, eating spots, bar, dive shops (no, not needed) and more out on the road nearby, pool and aircon as standard, and a Thai massage studio attached to delight Anne. Outrigger boats were parked on the beach outside the hotels and guesthouses lining the beachfront, and more warungs again, in bright colourings.

'Take two.'

At mid-morning, he took her to the Cup Resto. His barista girl from months back was not there.

'Just **kopi Bali**,' he said. Pique. Or nostalgia at work.

The coffees were slow. Three sturdy young lads came with much noise from the beach end of the shop, past them onto the street front ahead of where they sat. The men huffed and panted, carrying with much effort a huge black fish.

'That's a marlin,' he said. 'How are they going to handle that?'

                    BALI in its MIDDLE AGES

'How DID they handle that? It must have come in on a jukung outrigger. Try hauling that aboard!'

The men phoned, fussed, argued, and then brought a large bike to the scene. Twenty minutes it took to get right, but that  marlin was loaded onto the motorbike, curled around on itself, roped on, and measured across-ways because its long bill was still left as a dangerous blade far out to the side of the bike.

As quickly as this scenario started, it finished. The motorbike drove, slowly, off along the street. Someone had gained an insane amount of food, or had made some fabulous money for the week.

At Pakel's, an outrigger was beached on the sand below them. It was tired, had lived a hard life. The paint was scored and peeling.

At early morning a young man arrived at the boat and carried his cans and tools. By late morning, his scraping on the paint had made that sad boat rather worse than before. He resumed later in the afternoon, when the sun was losing its strength.

'Hey, it's lost its floats. Look.'

And it had. The bamboo pontoons lay like long battered logs beside the stranded boat. The wide spider legs that hold the outriggers now had no feet.

In three days of careful caulking, preparation and painting, days of paint and solvent smells wafting about, that jukung was transformed. Its outrigger floats looked good but still sat on the sand.

'Spiffy!' she said.

'That's technical?'

'No, but it is spiffy.'

'Agreed.'

She went downstairs to order a lime juice and a Bali coffee. What was delivered ten minutes later was two lime juices and his coffee.

'Yang mana tanpa gula?'

The warung man pointed to one of the juices. 'Ini.'

            BALI in its MIDDLE AGES

She pointed to the other. 'And with sugar?'

'Ya.'

'OK, 'kasih.'

'Huh?' said Jack.

She picked up her one, the unsweetened one, sipped it to check, then took the normal sweetened juice and walked down to the boatman to offer him the drink.

Jack did a fast calculation. Ramadan keeps moving each year. Was it Ramadan now? This is a coastal man, so he might be Muslim. But no, Ramadan was earlier in the year. He relaxed and watched.

This was too far away to hear the conversation, so after a while he left his coffee to join them.

'This is Gede Jono,' she said. 'His father died last month, and this was his father's boat. Jono is going to use it with a diving school. He is getting married soon, and must support his family.'

The man resumed his work in the heat of the afternoon, and they retreated to their shade on their balcony.

This story sounds familiar, he thought.

'Did you see he had a crucifix around his neck?'

Kristen, Katolik.

The floats went back on next morning. That took a while. The fixing was done with a strong polyester twine, and then some more filler for the joint edges. More paint. Clean up. Job done.

'The only thing left untouched, painted around, was his old logo,' he said, looking down as dark was approaching.

'You're right. "**Kadek si Raja Laut**". King of the Sea. Plus that artistic blue fish.'

There was a Kadek Homestay down the road. Or was Kadek his father?

'And look at the tiny bits of trim colour.' Like many of the boats, the hull and outriggers were in bright white. But every boat had its variation on the small bands of colour. Always primary colour, strong red or blue or green. Jono's trim was red and blue, exactly where the bamboo pontoons were tied on.

'If you were an anxious partner watching which boats were coming home, you would need good eyes.'

The morning they left Amed, the boat had gone.

———

As always, to Ubud, where the airport trip was then short.

Anne has the skill to start a conversation with a dog, a baby, the baby's mother, anyone in a coffee shop. And with any person in Bali, because two languages can give more options.

But this woman in the burka was Arabic. Or her book had a title in Arabic. It might not work. She sat at the next table, in the tea shop downhill on the right along Jalan Raya.

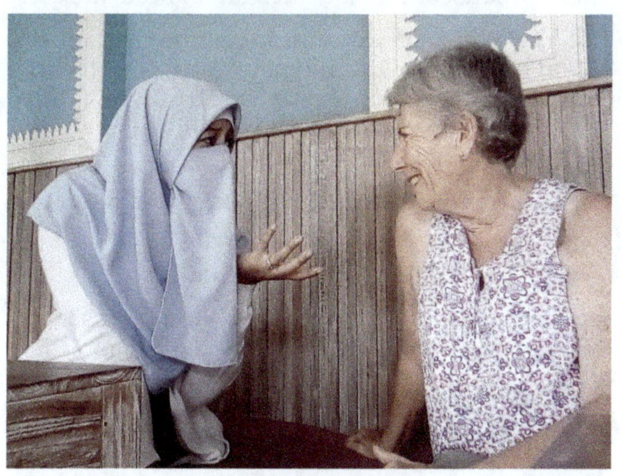

In Lombok, a simple hijab head covering was not uncommon, just an option. In Bali even that head-scarf was rare. But there was not ever a burka.

'Hello,' tried Anne.

'Hello. What a wonderful day out there.'

A remarkable and spirited ninety-minute conversation followed. He was impressed.

Jazmin was Libyan, but for a year now had lived in Jakarta. She was a reporter or academic correspondent at a conference being held in Ubud that week. The subject? "LGB and Homosexuality in the Muslim Cultures".

They all paused. Then, 'That's an allowed subject?'

'But yes. We want to understand our humanness. "Go about the earth, see how He originated His creation." We should know the truth in all the world. Some people are different but we need tolerance and love, all of us.'

They each ordered another tea. It gave a pause.

And those eyes peering out! The lure and the myth of the Arab eyes, alive and dark.

The one question they were not game to ask was whether she was counting herself as somewhere on that great rainbow. It was too hard to judge whether that might be too personal, or even dangerous to be speaking aloud.

This was a discussion he had never expected to be in.

———

At Denpasar Airport they were surprised to see many staff and some passengers wearing blue paper face masks. Indonesia's authorities were

BALI in its MIDDLE AGES

still insisting that no SARS had been detected in their country.

By ten days after the two travellers had arrived home, Australia had closed itself from the world.

—— —— ——

Rebecca called him one evening during the pandemic lockdowns—that long and wasted era of QR codes and masks.

'Hello, favourite daughter,' he spoke back to the phone. 'How are you enjoying these freezing winter Canberra nights?'

'Oh, Dad, it's always cold nights. Tonight will be minus three.'

'Have you been out to the Collector farm this year to gather wood for your fire?'

'Once, and I bought a local ute-load as well. Then I don't have to chop the wood to fit in the fireplace.'

Rebecca had grown up in Canberra and, besides her major overseas assignments some years, had never left. The house in Canberra and the bushland acres forty kilometres away in Collector were hers, both courtesy of her mother's will.

'You still going in to work on the Vespa scooter?'

'Sure. Most days.'

She's crazy, he thought. My daughter.

'When I do go, that is. I work from home a lot. The office is empty except for a couple of bosses and some IT geeks keeping us connected.'

She paused.

'Dad, I am ringing for a reason. Tonight I got home from work, and I had a strange envelope in my letterbox. It had your name on it—just Jack.'

'Yeah?'

'And a few minutes ago, your old mate Ben rang me. He had dropped it in my box today, he said. Christy had called him, old Christy in the wheelchair, and it had arrived to her in the mail from overseas.'

'Mystery,' he said. 'Read me what you can see.'

'What I have is a regular letter envelope, but he said Christy received it inside a larger envelope. It had included a note, hoping she had sent it to the right person called Christy or Kristie after so many years. And it had this envelope for "Jack".'

'"She", you said, "she" had sent it to Christy?'

'Yes, Ben said it that way.'

'Well, I wasn't sure if Christy was still alive. I hadn't heard of her for a long time.'

'She still does some personal counselling. So an internet search might have shown something.'

'And by now, Christy would not know how to contact me. She should know old hippie grandfather Ben though. Or how to reach him.' Ben still lived in his ancient farmhouse and land past Queanbeyan.

Rebecca saw Ben occasionally too. She was lifelong friends, across several countries, with both of Ben's daughters. The kids had had many childhood adventures in common when Jack and Ben knocked around together.

'So read the envelope.'

'OK. It says "For Jack of Canberra. Personal". That's all.'

'Nothing about who from, except it's a woman?'

'Correct.'

Should he ask Rebecca to open it? Or to mail it on?

Terry:

Dear Jack,

I'm sorry. I've been sorry for so long. My time is limited now, and I want to apologise to you before I am gone.

I am sending this into the world to find you. I believe it will find you. I need it to find you.

I did have to leave, and I couldn't tell you that so long ago in Bali. I can't spell out how that all happened, but the story I did tell you then wasn't quite the truth.

I need now to unburden myself for the confusion and hurt I know must have been there.

                    BALI in its MIDDLE AGES

I ran far across the world to where I was born, and where I still had my birth identity papers. I made a fresh life. Please know our night in Legian was part of my transition. Thank you.

My new life has been happy, eventually, and I have made a family with a tribe now of adorable grandchildren and already one great-granddaughter. I do trust you have found your own comforts and happiness.

My Regards,

"Terry"

After the Plague

On April Fool's Day, Jack was dispatched without notice to Brisbane for a cardiac bypass operation.

A few days later, before he had even left hospital, Anne had delivered to the airline the "Can't Travel" signature from the surgeon. The Bali airfare, a booking for next week, was converted to a credit voucher. She then succeeded in cancelling the only committed accommodation booking, at Seminyak.

So the travel insurance company now had no claims to pay out against and no travel to cover, and they repaid most of the insurance premium. That was unexpected.

Post-covid Bali had to wait for a later date.

Seminyak hadn't existed as any tourist place. But then Legian village had not been there once, either.

Yes, Legian, the emerging Legian beyond old Kuta. Kuta and Deanna. Legian and Christy. Legian and

"Terry", Terry in alias quote marks, no address, and endless questions. So long ago, he thought, so much change to Bali over the years. So much change in him too. So what was Seminyak?

Rebecca worked now for a prestigious events company. Six months ago she had a confidential mission in Europe, lasting a few weeks. Immediately after, to decompress, she hid away alone in a villa at Seminyak. Her reports to home of the food, the shopping, the bars, the sunsets and the long walks were enthusiastic, not this time any secret.

She came home with an offer. 'Dad, let's go together. I'm shouting you both to the best coffee and the best Italian food you can find.'

Italian?

Alas, her job schedules didn't work out. The joint trip hadn't happened yet. It became a trip for two, but to include this Seminyak. The free Italian meal deal still stood.

Then it became a trip for no one, as chronicled above.

Spring was coming now, he still lived, his ribcage had been wired up and rested, and the airline credit voucher had paid for fresh Bali flight tickets.

———

On Sunday, for no special reason, they walked into the sunshine, past the marathon runners doing their "annual" on the closed-off streets outside, up alongside the Maroochy River through Cotton Tree Park, with its usual weekend family groups and escooter speedsters. At the Sunshine Plaza bus station, they caught the 620 bus, one of the new electric ones, and watched the glorious late winter glide past as they wound their way through the suburbs to Coolum Beach.

'Now, coffee,' she said.

'Or a frosty Bintang?'

'Stop it,' she said. 'We don't fly there for another two weeks.'

'Twelve days,' he said.

It was a good coffee, from a hole-in-the-wall. They fought their way, J-walking, across the busy main road, and took their coffees across to the grassed parkland fronting the surf beach. Scores of people were about, sitting on the grass, down swimming in today's small waves, sunbaking on the white sand, or strolling and looking at everything.

Coolum is more laid-back than others of the beachside towns along here. A holiday atmosphere. The trees are broad, giving a lot of shade for lounging around. Many birds, kookaburra, crows, magpies, were scratching in the grass and in the bark mulch for their food,

  BALI in its MIDDLE AGES

and some were pestering and swooping past the picnickers.

They sat a while to watch the world, and then wandered for an hour up the wooden boardwalk built some years ago by the Council. The Coolum Boardwalk is renowned and popular. It leads to the top of the Point Arkwright sea cliff, and there it is yet another spot to stop, look, absorb and cogitate slowly. And to help some visitors take their stunning group photo to post or brag about later.

Back sitting on the 620, Anne finished that comment. 'Yes, the Bali Bintang would work.'

Then this: 'Do you want us to walk Legian again to try to find your first places?'

Legian, that new Kuta once.

He and Anne had been together to Legian just once in their travels, but the Legian stories were known.

His answer was No.

And Kuta? Double No.

'But let's go see Seminyak. Walk Seminyak.'

Seminyak and Anne?

Seminyak, before it's all superseded in its turn by next-along Canggu. Or were they too late already?

———

Anne volunteers each week at the local Neighbourhood Community Centre. She came in after this morning's gathering. 'I was talking about Bali with one of the mothers,' she said.

'Martha had her wedding a few years ago at a place in Nusa Dua. Sometimes on their anniversary they go back. Next year they are taking their two young kids.'

'Always the same place?'

'Always there. But she was concerned it was so expensive, $800 a night. Her husband is the only earner.'

'800? For $800 we could stay for more than two weeks in the Seminyak place we booked.'

'I know. I showed her some pictures on my phone. Good rooms, good pool. Restaurant. It was an eye-opener to her. She's gone home to do some more online research.'

So much that has been upsold, he thought. It's like being persuaded you need a $2000 phone versus a $350 one.

———

Their Seminyak hotel, 24-hour, all serviced, pool, the lot, was no resort, but it was a good pick, a block from "Eat Street" and "The Square" one way, and a block from the beach the other way.

    BALI in its MIDDLE AGES

The airport pickup, Made, booked as a booking.com extra on the room booking—and how easy was that?—had made slow travel, as the traffic was so choked.

'Don't remember that,' she said wheeling her bag in and bypassing the doorman with a wave. 'Never traffic like that before.'

First, see the local beach, Petitenget Beach. A forlorn creek ran along and then turned to sea, so they crossed the stone-work bridge past the traffic guards into the vehicle park. The creek stank and was full of rubbish. The last good cleaning flow must have been at some earlier season, but then pity the sea. They walked through another Balinese stone bridge onto the sand.

'There's no one here,' she said. Almost no one.

One hand-cart offered a "Quicky". They looked again. A coffee.

Petitenget Beach had zero charisma. Not being the surfer, he nearly forgot to look at the breaks, but then decided the Maroochydore surf at home could outplay these waves of today.

They battled the traffic again—'Not as bad as Hanoi,' he said—and they found their way past the Mexicola nightclub to Seminyak Square. The Square was the complete, if small, suburban mall with top familiar brands and well-glassed ultra-clean shops.

On the street were the occasional café, lots of art and trend-wear shops, but no sign of any place looking like an Indonesian food warung.

But it was a SIM and phone shop they were seeking, a **Toko Celular**. A counter-in-the-corridor had to do, near a nightspot they had been cautioned on.

The local SIM was fitted to Anne's phone, and that would be their hotspot for when wifi was not available or was too flaky. Now they were ringable, textable, online as a local. It was time to call cousin Julie, staying in Kuta tonight, said facebook, but flying out tomorrow.

　　　　　BALI in its MIDDLE AGES

'Drinks and eating in Kuta? Sure. What time?'

At six. Already it was four. Through that traffic? They hurried back to the hotel and talked with the doorman.

'My brother,' he said. 'Let me call him. Will you go on his motorbike?'

They looked at each other. On the insurance this time, he hadn't ticked motorbike riding. Was being pillion a risk?

'We live once,' she said.

'Both with your brother?' Jack said to the doorman.

That was ignored. 'You both want a helmet?'

Shit, yeah.

It took 50 minutes through the narrow roads close to the beach, south through Seminyak/Petitenget, Seminyak proper, Double-6, Legian and Kuta. No car could pass on such narrow roads, only bikes, surging over each speed hump in turn.

He kept peeping around Anne's helmet, and then knocking the helmets together as a semaphore. No, that alarmed her.

He held grimly to the frame under his bottom, because the real pillion seat was sized for one pillion passenger, not two. He was perched on that metal frame that every bike had extending behind the padded seat, "just in case". Not quite legal, he presumed, but so obvious.

The driver had no helmet—Anne wore that one.

Was he getting too old for pranks like this? But it was only ten years ago he and Anne had sped across the Mekong Delta as pillion on two bikes, their tiny cabin backpacks on their own backs, and their two checked-luggage trolley bags held vertically in front of each driver in his foot space.

'Jack, you forgot Mushroom Beach.' He had.

Onto Jalan Legian and to the old Bemo Corner. Surprise! To this day the intersection still had a Balinese "thing" standing in the middle, if nothing else was familiar.

Their driver was paid off, then they slipped past the Kartika Plaza security guards to find Julie in that huge, elegant foyer.

'You're late,' she said. 'Hello, Cuz.'

They were late back home that night to Seminyak, too. The brain rebelled—this morning they had been still in Brisbane.

Seminyak's Petitenget Beach got exonerated. Approaching sunset on the weekend it was a hive of activity, families, kids, tourists, kite-fliers and a few touts. People stood and watched, some pushed kids on the swing, some cocktailed on a beanbag, some picnicked their own event on a rug

                    BALI in its MIDDLE AGES

on the grey sand. The dogs joined in the soccer practice and two riders on horseback trotted past and then back.

The sun set quickly in that west, and a thousand families stacked onto a thousand motorbikes from the parking lot and merged back into the night streets.

Next day, they walked Eat Street to past a substantial nightclub. The rumours had suggested foreign agents could be on seduction patrol nearby at dark, but it looked to them like a fashionable, expensive club. That is, not their sort of place after dark to be finding out.

They walked everywhere else also. That had been Rebecca's secret formula for Seminyak before them. Don't think of driving or riding anywhere. Just walk, walk, walk more. Double-6 and Legian Beaches they found down the same narrow tracks the doorman's brother had taken them.

Thus began their warung hunt. "The Best Warung in Seminyak?" The online reviews said Waroeng Bernadette, and they found it nestled in the flea market. Go for his sought-for rendang, the good version, a Sumatran Padang dish, tender and fibrous and long-cooked. Across the next table, they saw it, a huge plateful of food, the diner struggling. They ordered just one for sharing.

'But this décor?' he whispered. It wasn't his old, simple, rustic "Original Bali". It was modern, well-glassed, hung with art. A European place with Indonesian food.

'Enjoy your **rendang**. That's what you came for.'

On the morrow, they walked north to Rebecca's stated favourite, Warung Eny, short of Canggu, and they sent Messenger shots to Canberra. She was at work, but the thumbs-up came straight back.

The order was a young coconut first, then **sate**, smoked over the coconut shells. Smoke drifted through.

'Ah, smells like the Jakarta satay man's fire at Darwin's Mindil Market,' she said.

On the return, they had passed two vape shops and two tattooists. Now they were sitting at the laneway corner south of the warung, still well up the high end of Seminyak.

'A gelato!' had said Anne. 'Yes.'

                    BALI in its MIDDLE AGES

He had stopped walking and looked at her with a feigned scorn.

'I don't care. I know it's no cheaper than at home, but I'm having one.'

So there they were now, sitting at that store bench on high wooden stools, facing the streets and the parade, and each licking on a gelato cone.

'That looks like a golf buggy coming on the lane,' she said.

The main street was noisy with motor traffic, and the road was itself a busy retail area with a lot of pedestrian traffic to the shops. At the lane corner, a large sign read "Peppers Resort 300m".

The large people-carrier buggy stopped beside them at the lane's end.

A man and a woman climbed out, awkward, unfit. They were well-dressed, in trousers, shirt, frock. The man sported a moustache in the caricatured way of a crusty English army colonel. For two minutes they stood as though bewildered, until a break in the traffic allowed them to hurry across the main road.

'What's their story, do you think?'

'Peppers' customers,' she said.

'That's obvious.'

He licked around the melting side, then looked up again. The old couple were getting into a Bluebird taxi. By twenty seconds later, the taxi was gone, the buggy car had headed back along the lane, and the world went back to normal.

'Scurried away. Well, now they're safe.'

'If you are living in that world inside a resort fence, you can't be in Bali,' she said.

'Yep. Same. If you can't walk and explore the streets and alleys, you're not in the Bali I know.'

They chewed down the cones and wondered what to do about sticky fingers. Sanitiser.

'No, let's stop,' she warned. 'Every one of us coming from elsewhere has to learn how we cope. It's not our country. We are all out of our place.'

Seminyak. Not their sort of place!

They didn't belong here. They never would belong. Not a correct fit.

Back in their room, she said, 'Not what it all once was, is it? Too much fashion. Top restaurants everywhere. Impossible traffic.'

'Hmmm. What is it? What is Bali? Or what was it? Go back before us, to the early surfers of Kuta and Uluwatu. Then look at this over-cooked Bali we have now. Polluted and crowded beyond control. We've all been, all us foreigners, the neo-colonialists and the spoilers. It never could have been something we had a dozen times for free.'

                    BALI in its MIDDLE AGES

She frowned. 'You are so dramatic.'

———

'Made,' he said, 'every car has a registration number starting with "DK". Explain that to me.'

Made had been their airport pickup driver a few days ago. They found him again using WhatsApp. Anne had installed WhatsApp because all the tourist trade, tourist clients and Balinese providers, all of them, now use it to make arrangements and deals. Facebook was past tense.

'Yes, that DK code is used for all cars and trucks and scooters in Bali. In Java and Sumatra and other islands, they have different letters.'

Made's car, a Toyota SUV, he rented. He kept it on hire at three million rupiah a month. 'I need the car, because it's my driver income,' he said.

'And the two letters at the end of the car's number,' continued Made, 'mean which area in Bali the car is licensed in. Big cities like Denpasar have a lot of area codes, and little towns one code.'

Jack calculated in his head the number of registration combinations. The four middle digits makes ten thousand for starters. The area codes, 26 letters x 26 letters, that's over 600. Total possible registration codes for Bali is about 6 million.

'How many people live in Bali?'

'More than 8 million.'

He looked at the traffic of cars and bikes. Most of the population was about on bikes.

'One day soon Bali will not have enough numbers.'

It was a nonsensical exercise. Let the planners do their organising. They get paid for it.

There were few trucks now. They had left behind the crowded Denpasar–Gilimanuk highway half an hour ago, and were climbing the mountain roads northwards.

Made pulled aside a while so they could watch a band of monkeys, many of them young, playing at the edge of the jungle at the roadside. Monkeys they had seen before, though, even on Lombok between Senggigi and the Gilis ferry. They moved on up the range.

Then he spotted a car with THREE final letters in its rego number. Now the possible combinations for Bali rose to 150 million. Bali was not going to be short of vehicle numbers.

'Jack, enjoy, turn off that brain.'

'Those are coffee trees,' said Made.

Jack wound down the window and snapped a hasty photo on his phone. It was blurry.

          BALI in its MIDDLE AGES

'We are coming into my home village.'

This was unexpected. Pupuan district.

'I was a boy here. My father grows coffee, a lot of coffee.'

Made pointed to the family cottage, an unpretentious place on the main road, and they didn't stop.

'I will stay there tonight, if the homestay room is empty.'

'Do you see your family often?'

'Every month or two. My father and sister. My mother is dead many years, from a fever.'

They drove in silence a while.

'This is too high now. Too cool for coffee.' Another pause. 'I liked living here more than Jimbaran. I lived near the city to study, but now I just drive.'

'Every day?'

'Every day. I like driving.'

'And now,' said Made, the local boy, 'we should have a lunch. The warung ahead is special. It serves a famous local rice entil in their meal, and they cook it for five hours.'

'Is it like sticky black rice? Like bubur injin the breakfast porridge?'

'A little. It's white rice cooked until the grains are dissolved, and it's pressed in seasoned leaves into cakes. It's like a **lontong**.'

They stopped at Warung Dedy in Sanda. "Entil Sanda" for three, and **kopi Bali**. Savoury gravy, coconut but not too spicy, some vegetables and the entil spiced lontongs. A $6 bill, including the driver's meal as per custom. All overlooking the mountain countryside. Bali. Then time to go.

They'd been manoeuvred. It's the game. It's not a bad game.

Half an hour later, as they crested the range, the north coast far ahead came into view.

———

Ibu Komang brought breakfast to the tiled veranda of the Putu Guesthouse.

The mountains were stark, visible to the south. The lush Balinese garden almost hid the path of concrete tiles cast from that ubiquitous grey volcanic-sand concrete. The house shrine, still always of angular concrete castings, was standing at the end, on it the morning offerings to the gods. And half-lost in the bushes was hanging a bell-shaped bamboo fighting cockerel cage, empty.

This was Pemuteran, a sleepy fishing village, offering diving and snorkelling activities and

     BALI in its MIDDLE AGES

accommodation for the few hardier tourists. Neither of them had been here before.

Komang placed the breakfast out on the low table. 'You have plan today?'

Komang could organise anything for a price.

'No plan. **Jalan jalan, dan jalan lagi,**' he said. 'We walk.'

She looked at him again. 'Oh, you wear **sarong**?'

He had intended bringing the flat one that worked well as a beach towel, but by error came with the sewn-around one that he had on now. Ikat.

'Sometimes,' he said.

'You buy here?'

'I bought it forty years ago.'

She looked disbelieving, or misunderstanding.

'**Membeli empat puluh tahun yang lalu,**' he repeated. Forty years.

'In Bali?'

'I forget. Maybe Bali. **Mungkin Jawa, mungkin Lombok.**'

He looked at his sarong. It had survived well. If the Dutch still ran this place, he might be deemed "gone native".

Many decades ago in Sydney, he had worn it around the house he was sharing with the lovely, gentle Donna. More other stories.

Donna's two kids, six and eight, had fled weeping to their mother. 'But Mum, men can't wear dresses.'

And how many, many times, too, was the sarong, his or theirs, needed for entry to a Balinese temple?

Komang walked off, and they were left to enjoy their breakfast and his No Plan.

No Plan became snorkelling at the BioRock electric-enhanced reef structure offshore, at the end of their lane, but the sea was murky. Only the two scuba divers wading back in could report anything useful.

Anne therefore booked a half-day boat tour tomorrow to Menjangan Island, half an hour on the water away.

'I'm sure they'll have swimming fins,' she said. 'At least I have my own face-mask and snorkel, rather than one from their communal bin.'

No, he had decided. He'd take a quiet day writing. The backpack and gear of the plane trip was still giving his post-op chest some aches. And then the walk-everywhere regime in Seminyak had left him with a swollen foot. A quick look around Doctor Google gave him "10 Things" (or 14) to start worrying over regarding a puffed foot. Getting older sucks.

'You go and enjoy.'

At the appointed 9 am, she stepped out, and right on time was driven off.

Three sentences was all he wrote that day. Sometimes, for a writer, an isolate, sitting with a drink in somewhere as innocently named as "Eco Taste Café" can be a dangerous risk. One might meet an energetic young Canadian couple, and spend five hours solving the world's problems and sharing a fish curry and a secret or three.

'Oh shit, I must go,' he said. 'Anne ought be home, and I have our room key.'

And it was indeed getting late. The bakso seller was already positioned for the evening at her usual spot across the road. What had happened to the old kaki lima push-carts? Her mini truck was fitted out as her mobile meatball kitchen and sales unit.

All four met again on the morrow, same Eco, and spent the same five hours all over.

Life can be like that. He feels younger.

Eco had a traveller bookshelf, but one tiny volume was signed by the authors and was not for removal. ***Secret Bali, An Unusual Guide***, by two French travellers. It was NOT anything like the handful of Lonely Planet and its kind. It's the book he wanted for keeping. Breaking the regular genre, and breaking every layout convention he worked to, ***Secret Bali*** was priceless. He wanted to write like that.

Four times to Bali he had carried a spare set of spectacles. This time it happened: the arm fell off

                    BALI in its MIDDLE AGES

his main ones, and the tiny screw vanished into the universe. The standby pair were old, to an old script. The world went blurry.

'Jack,' said Putu, 'let me help.' He disappeared a few minutes and returned with a kit of mini drivers and an old pair of sunglasses, broken. But with its two screws.

The world reappeared.

To a festivals veteran, moon phases are always relevant. Tomorrow, they should walk up the mountain track in the moonlight and watch the sun-break from the temple.

———

Putu drove them to Lovina, that stretch of fifteen kilometres of beach, the holiday strip out of nearby Singaraja, the capital. But there are still a few very central streets at Kalibukbuk village, housing the hippie-tourist boutique guesthouses and funky warungs and tokos selling feathers and trinkets. And the Greco Café on the corner, that highway junction with the one-only traffic lights, the lampu lintas. That Kalibukbuk touro enclave had been their target.

'We have gone too far,' said Putu. 'I must turn back,' and he made a 6-point turn on the highway.

'Putu, my map says we turn by the Greco.' That was on the Agoda map screenshot on his tablet.

Putu ignored this and followed his live map on his phone. The Wahyu Danu Hotel was 3 kilometres back on the main road but still fronting the sea to its north.

'Oh,' said the receptionist, 'the booking agencies have three different wrong locations for where we are supposed to be. And your booking coming through Agoda is happening more often. We have a contract only with booking.com, and we have learned to accept bookings only where you pay us on arrival.'

Moral: don't trust any map. Don't trust the booking systems. They work together, on their own side, not necessarily your side.

Wahyu Danu was signed on its street board as 4-star. Probably it once was. It was a grand little place, including an infinity pool and a spacious conference room boasting a huge chandelier.

'Past glory,' said Anne. 'From me, one star now.'

'But it's a formula.'

Covid times had cruelled many spots in Bali. Not all the tourists had returned.

'And remember, high season finished last week.' Of the 7 prime rooms and a dozen others, only two rooms were occupied. The outdoor restaurant had staff and skill left for only breakfast or a nasi goreng.

Over the beach wall was a littered black volcanic sand strip. Frustrated hawkers prowled the beach calling over the wall.

On the first morning, early, with the seaboard mosque still calling, an old man approached an unsuspecting Anne outside their room and struck up a conversation in Indonesian.

Let's call him Ho Chi Minh, because his face and his white, wispy beard were a good look-alike. When the penny dropped that he wanted to sell flowers, the transaction was wound up.

'He was a kindly old man, though,' said Anne.

Walk to Lovina central. Revisit their old haunts from another year. Drink real coffee at the Greco. A good plan for the day.

The internet had fingered the Greco as the spot to target. 'I reckon that Greco corner is where we were let out by the Tirta Gangga driver the other time we came here.'

'What, ten years ago?'

'Longer?'

'Well, better start walking.'

The road, hotels on the left, and warungs—grilled fish all of them—and rice-fields inland on the south, had no footpaths and no safe space to be walking. They stuck to the left side.

'Should we walk on the right, to watch oncoming traffic?'

'No, we'll be right,' he replied.

Not fifty metres on, there was a loud metallic crash right behind them. Two motorbikes, one separate helmet and three bodies skidded in a tangle along the bitumen road past them, one metre to their right.

The first to get to his feet was a young lad, the only one now with a helmet still on. He clutched his shin in pain, but there was no apparent blood.

Jack stepped back to wave a warning to oncoming traffic until the roadway was cleared enough.

Bapak Ho, old man HC Minh, had stood up and was now berating the youth, demanding he reveal himself by removing the full-face helmet.

'Jack, we should leave. We can't be constructive.'

They left the scene with the two broken bikes beside the road, and Pak Ho consoling the careless

                    BALI in its MIDDLE AGES

perpetrator, now with his helmet off and bawling into Pak Ho's shoulder. The kid looked fifteen.

Too fast. Confidence of youth, carrying a pillion even. Clipped the old man's bike from behind. It happens so fast.

'Saw a young girl killed by a car in southern Bali about 35 years ago,' he said. 'Walk the other side?'

'Yes.'

Approaching dusk, they had returned to their hotel, ready to watch the sun setting straight out to sea. Happy hour for two. Only one more room looked occupied.

Sharing a Bintang, they sat in the beach pavilion and watched the house kitten yearning after a gecko up higher and out of reach on the pillar.

'I haven't seen a **cikcak** now for many a Bali trip,' he said.

'They freak out the tourists too much.'

He watched her holding the bottle. There was that tremor again in her hand. It had alarmed him so much once.

'Genetic,' she had said. 'Benign, familial, from my father. I'll likely always have that.'

But some very old memories still crept back to haunt him. Our grip on our sound heath, our claim to life itself, were never a promise to us from anywhere, and meantime our best response was to be howling with joy and energy. The sun was long, low, red. He looked into her face.

Several jukung outriggers sat offshore, and one with a pile of netting on deck was on the sand. Could they be props set there to entice travellers to stay and be impressed?

Two yells called down the beach, and several people appeared as by magic spell and rushed to shove the beached boat out to sea.

'Hey, you watching this?'

She turned in her seat to watch the commotion.

The jukung had no motor fitted. No propellor-on-a-stick was brought out, neither the noisy petrol type they had seen many of in the Mekong Delta, nor anything new, electric and quiet. Instead a dozen bodies waded into the water, pushing their boat so it sat a hundred and fifty metres away in front of where he and Anne were being tourist-passive.

By now there were fifteen eager Balinese bodies around the boat. Still at a standing depth they cast their net wide, then, relentless and purposeful, they shook it in unison and drew it ever tighter for a 20-minute well-practised routine. Finally, with a lot of effort, they dragged the net and its catch aboard.

                    BALI in its MIDDLE AGES

The boat came back and nine buckets of fish were carried to the sand. A crowd gathered. Family—they presumed it was family—got the first choices. The remaining buckets, standing on the sand beside the boat, were then subject to loud bidding.

'Ikan Bakar warungs buy,' said the hotel woman who was watching with them. She pointed streetwards, eastwards.

Buckets went off in several directions. The Balinese crowd dispersed.

'You hungry yet?' he asked. The sun was falling into the sea of the horizon, and then only the dying glow remained. The dark would not be long.

'Bring a torch,' she said. 'I'm following the grilled fish. They'll have another Bintang there, no doubt.'

Roar with joy.

———

Onwards. For a few days, Anne snorkelled straight off the black sand beach at Amed, under the volcano. This time they had secured lodging at exactly the "central" spot, Blue Star Bungalows and Café at Jemeluk Bay.

Ah, this was the closest they had been to that apocryphal perfect holiday place. Food, drink, ocean, warmth, lounges, view from bed.

On the snorkelling, he demurred again, citing "rehab". He read and wrote.

They walked up to Pakel's, their accommodation in Amed last time. Kadek the masseuse was still running her massage clinic there.

'I still prefer the Thai mode. It's dearer than the usual Bali massage, but compared to home it still is an amazing cheap massage.'

Kadek made the room call twice to Anne at Blue Star.

Some evenings Blue Star featured a happy hour, $8 cocktails—local spirit—served then as two for one. But her gin and tonic, to "keep you company", was not "local", didn't qualify for discount.

'Our arak is very good,' promised the waiter. 'Guarantee, my family made it.'

Jack didn't die.

Then only three nights remained before the flight out. Somewhere in the south, as usual, would suit.

Sanur? 'Boring,' he said.

'Uluwatu?' he countered. No reply.

Legian?

It wasn't working.

But not Kuta. Never Kuta with those noisy Aussies.

'Ubud, as we always do?'

'Reputation is gone to ruin, traffic impossible. Rumour says it's like Phuket, filling with Russians, who are worse than the Australians.'

A driver agreed on 500,000 rupiah to take them to Poppy's Lane in Kuta. Poppy's Lane 1—when did more Poppy's Lanes appear?

Daughter back home: 'Huh? You doing some new social experiment?'

They were sitting at the Blue Star café table next to the sand. Several jukung were two hundred metres out, past the coral, and their passengers were in the water snorkelling. It was high tide.

'But that's our reef.'

From the left, another boat approached, angling its way to the beach, trying to stay inshore of the coral. It ran to sand in front of them, and its two passengers stepped ashore and walked to the café counter, leaving the boatman to pull out a light rope.

'Hey, hey, look …' He stood to peer at the boat. 'That's, that's—'

'That's Gede Jono.' She bounded out to talk to him.

Jack had spotted the logo, the one they had admired four years ago. But only Anne would ever have that instant recall of names and stories.

The boat was easily left safe for a short visit, and Jono, after figuring out who was this bule woman accosting him, then was happy to accept a local coffee for himself.

'Married now? How wonderful. Anak?'

'I have one already, anak perempuan. I love her. And soon another.'

'Punya foto?'

   BALI in its MIDDLE AGES

He beamed, and from a scruffy wallet he drew a small photo of his two women.

Anne fussed; she wanted the whole story. She got a whole story. The Balinese love stories of family.

The couple having their shore break politely signalled they were finished. Jono panicked.

'Tomorrow, you can come in my boat to the reef?'

'Jono, thank you,' he said, 'thank you. We must say no. Sorry. Tomorrow early we leave Amed. You tell your wife you love her. Tell her she looks very pretty.'

All shook hands. A Western goodbye.

———

Slip back five years. It was a philosophic discussion group, meeting each week, making friends, sharing ideas. The group called themselves "In Praise of Idleness", in homage to a short work a century ago by the Brit Bertrand Russell.

They were all approximately idlers, retired, still keeping some mental life ticking over. The Idleness group ran energetic discussions, argumentative, feisty.

Location: Jack's lounge room. Week's subject: The flâneur. The flâneuse, the street explorer.

Idlers:

No, I go for a walk to keep my heart healthy. Three times a week along Alex Headland foreshore and to Mooloolaba Spit and back.

Ah, I should be doing that more often, too. I have one stent already.

Yes, but they say—yes, "they do say"—that exercise is a resistance against encroaching dementia, too.

Murmurs of approval among the greyheads.

So what's this idea of just strolling, wandering the streets without a purpose?

French bohemian-era bullshit. Poets inventing an attractive lifestyle when they are extolling laziness.

No, I get it, I think. Sure, do your exercise. Swim, walk, do bicep curls with cans of mango. But sometimes going slow, exploring what's around you, taking the time to observe things, noting things you hadn't seen before—I get that. Things that are right near you every day. The connoisseur of slums and beggars and birds, maybe of old London streets or Paris.

Old Europe, nothing. We live right here. Ever spotted the increasing number of homeless hidden still asleep in the bushes near here if you get out to walk early enough? It makes me want to volunteer at the Neighbourhood Centre's free meals nights.

Who has noticed the thousands of flowers in the cotton trees in the park by the Maroochy River here this year? I think it's because of all the rain now after the dry years. I get out there for strolls.

Me too. I go out walking some days not knowing where I'll get to. I discovered a narrow laneway last week, a track towards the beach. It's not far from home, but in ten years I'd never noticed it. And you ought to have seen some of the graffiti down along it on the fence. Nothing like it. Small and artistic. I had to take a shot to brag about later.

So, it's the experience, stupid?

———

The one-way beach road Jalan Pantai past Bemo Corner, the earliest remnant of last century's surfer-touro Bali, was clogged to that same slow, slow crawl that was strangling Seminyak. The newer beachfront road was worse. Poppy's Lane 1 is then too narrow to allow car traffic right through, only endless scooters.

His mind's eye looked back to a Bali streetscape with a lot of people walking, a few old Dutch style pushbikes when the kids were leaving school, and the occasional motorbike or bemo. But Indonesians don't walk now.

So on this early afternoon they dragged their trolley bags along the cobbles of the lane, dodging bikes. Most of the tiny shopfronts were shut. Several large property sites had been demolished and fenced off, awaiting a later more flourishing year.

The Fat Yogi Bungalows was old Kuta, but was still kept clean and functional. Or the visible 40% of the premises was.

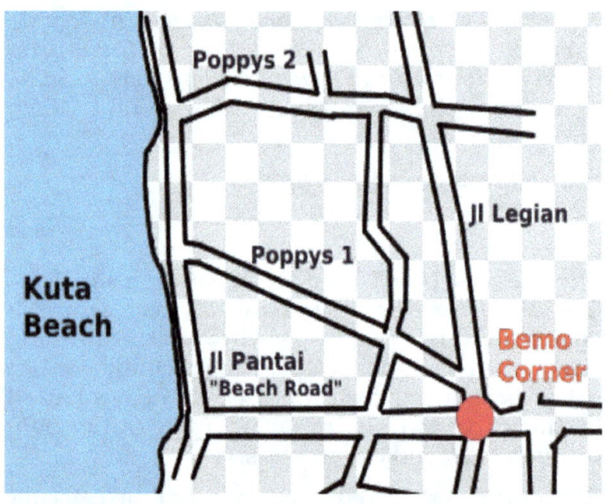

He got suspicious. Back shortly, he said.

Behind the Reception was a door ajar, and a huge downstairs concrete-roofed dungeon could be seen. Rubbish was littered all over. Had it been

                    BALI in its MIDDLE AGES

once garaging space? Above that was an equally large hall. Entertainment hall? A "Fat Yogi" yoga premises? Above that again was a large mezzanine floor, suggestive of a substantial church choir loft. His best guess was still the yoga originally, but long ago.

Or was it an abandoned nightclub floor and parking space underneath?

He climbed the nearby old, tiled stairs into an adjoining 2-storey wing building. It had about 20 rooms along the bleak corridors, all looking long unoccupied. Conference or yoga retreat attendees?

The abandoned accommodation wing had a long frontage to Poppy's that included several trader shops, but all, except for one displaying a collection of offensive car stickers, were closed today or unoccupied. This wing also had a derelict "back yard" on its other side.

He retraced, and walked along a half-hidden path behind the no-walls breakfast dining area. Three decrepit bungalows were hidden there, hovels, one possibly sleeping someone. The others, through their windows, showed untidy stacks of old mattresses and furniture, and they were surrounded by rusty wheelbarrow and tools.

He walked back to their room. It was fine. The pool was well-kept and inviting and the gardens were typical tropic, lush Bali gardens. The illusion was complete.

That old colonel and his wife from Peppers Resort in Seminyak, terrified leaving their enclave and entering "Bali" for a moment? Jack thought of himself enjoying his poolside spot at Poppy's Lane. The two experiences were different in degree, but was there any difference in type?

Anne sat beside the pool, chatting in Indo and Anglo with a Balinese couple, their three kids and an Australian woman, Janet. Two of the kids were twins, and twins were common and cherished in Anne's own family.

By fifteen minutes later, the family had gone home, and Janet walked past their room.

'I normally live in your room. It had another booking this time, and I like my new room better now.'

'You live here?'

'Well, for the last few years I do, two months here and two weeks back in my flat in Perth.' She lived on her Australian Government pension. Ate daily at the nearest warung, Bamboo Corner.

'But I love being here with these people.'

'The children were comfortable with you.'

                    BALI in its MIDDLE AGES

'I've known them since they were all born. I'm called "Oma" usually.' Nanna. Dutch colonial word.

Janet had lived abroad for forty years, working in China, Russia, Vietnam and other difficult places, and raised her family of seven at the same time.

'But so amazing,' said Anne. 'Your husband?'

'We were a team.'

'What were you doing?'

'Both surgeons. We went to hotspots and catastrophes; we worked for WHO. A few years ago, he was doing a rescue surgery underground in Vietnam and the mine tunnel collapsed, and he never came out.'

Janet didn't blink.

'I decided to retire then. My kids are independent now. I have no money. I never had money, and I don't need it. So I live here."

'You need to be writing a book on that life,' he said.

'Nah, my kids can write the book. They lived through it all, saw many of the surgery jobs live in the field with us. Three are following in our footsteps.'

'That life,' said Anne. 'The drama. Are you missing it now?'

'Here in Bali, I'm still on call at several hospitals, when a job is tricky or urgent. Once or twice a week, I have a theatre job or some consultancy.'

'And who pays you?'

'No pay. It's not allowed on my tourist visas. I get a $15 per fortnight allowance from WHO. I'm happy.'

She went off to her own room and returned with a large hand of very green bananas.

'A friend gave me two lots of these,' she said. 'Too many. Please enjoy them when they ripen.'

'Oh, wow, thank you so much,' he said.

But in two days they would be in Queensland.

Last Bali?

———

'Walk down Poppy's again with me. I want to see Kuta Beach once more. I want to go slow and look.'

They walked out past a cart selling from a Chinese wok.

'Dahu goreng,' he said. 'Fried tofu cubes. That I've not seen for forty years. When we got too hungry, Christy and I used to eat this, piping hot, wrapped in torn-up newspaper. Even my Becc.'

Ten minutes later: 'These massive hotels here opposite the beach. The nightclub dancing with Deanna and Rebecca was along here, but I can't recognise anything.'

Anne had met Deanna in Melbourne many years ago. Met Christy once in Canberra, too. No secrets.

'Sliding doors,' she said.

'Very much so. Life had other possibilities. We takes our picks.'

'And we get to live with our picks.'

Deanna had married a Javanese man, had a son there, and returned after four years to Melbourne alone, very alone.

'I said, we each learn to live with our choices. We have to learn.'

'Can I have you?'

Boleh!

So that much looked a yes.

But they still had some promise outstanding, that they go together to Borobodur.

Outbound

A voyager's chronicle is the complete opposite of a travel guidebook, although neither can claim a story plot.

A guidebook—despite its precise facts—describes future tense, plans or dreams of what might happen, what we wish we could create. Dreams are made with the eyes still closed.

A logbook presents the past tense, what really happened, the washup. Most especially, it exposes people, insights, humour, luck, irony and effort, even attitude, and all dimensions of the unexpected, grief and joy. The wider were the eyes, the more might be revealed and enjoyed in the words.

There's another thing. A good guidebook ought be complete with all the reader might want, and then more. But the content of a log book is the writer's call. It gets just what the writer felt was worth the ink.

What is ink?

The Author

Brian Lavery was born in Sydney, a few hours before that first atomic bomb. That's what he blames, anyway.

He's been a monk, a teacher, a hippie, a nomad, a rebel, a corporate geek, a trainer, a world traveller, and now an idler.

He tried surviving Melbourne, Canberra and Darwin, but he settled in Queensland with Anne, and he wonders where all those years went.

Also by Brian Lavery

Down to Earth

Cassini's Vision

And published by Brian Lavery:

White Dawn, author John J Lee

And NOT published by Brian Lavery:

Hard Landing—a Down to Earth unpublished edition with zillions of photos, some not taken by him—because getting all the clearances is too daunting!

Bookmaker—a very detailed guide on using free software to prepare all text and cover files for self-publishing—but it still had a few errors to rewrite, and the technology kept changing underfoot.

Old Tales, author John J Lee—printed for family, with SKU number, not ISBN code that public distribution requires.

Cassini's Mission—the masterpiece is not written yet.